Structuring Drama Work

3rd edition

Jonothan Neelands and Tony Goode

CAMBRIDGE
UNIVERSITY PRESS

CAMBRIDGE
UNIVERSITY PRESS

University Printing House, Cambridge CB2 8BS, United Kingdom

One Liberty Plaza, 20th Floor, New York, NY 10006, USA

477 Williamstown Road, Port Melbourne, VIC 3207, Australia

4843/24, 2nd Floor, Ansari Road, Daryaganj, Delhi – 110002, India

79 Anson Road, #06–04/06, Singapore 079906

Cambridge University Press is part of the University of Cambridge.

It furthers the University's mission by disseminating knowledge in the pursuit of education, learning and research at the highest international levels of excellence.

Information on this title: education.cambridge.org

First published 1990
Third edition 2015
20 19 18 17 16 15 14 13 12 11 10 9 8 7 6

Printed in Great Britain by CPI Group (UK) Ltd, Croydon CR0 4YY

A catalogue record for this publication is available from the British Library

ISBN 978-1-107-53016-4 Paperback

Contents

Introduction

Note on the 25th Anniversary Edition

Since the first edition of *Structuring Drama Work* in 1992, there have been significant developments in the social and artistic uses of theatre and drama. We have tried to reflect these changes in this new edition. We have added new conventions to make 100 available here and have recognised the all-pervasive impact of the digital world in our cultural connections for each convention.

We have also, in our vocabulary and use of examples, sought to recognise the growth of applied theatre in a range of contexts from social justice programmes to business and corporate education. Participatory forms of applied theatre have grown from the same foundations of socially committed, educational and inquiry-based art that is the inspiration for *Structuring Drama Work*.

The idea of 'ensemble' as a guiding principle for the making and sharing of theatre that is based in social relationships and co-creation has taken hold in both the artistic theatre and in socially engaged applied theatre and drama work. *Structuring Drama Work* is based in these same principles and the very idea of conventions assumes an 'ensemble' approach to the making of meanings in social circumstances. We have thus strengthened and made explicit the ensemble foundations in this new edition.

The purpose of this book is to outline some of the conventions that are available to participants engaged in structuring dramatic activity; whether it be an improvisation or devising workshop, an active exploration of a text and its meanings, or a participatory workshop structured for others. In addition, the book sets out models for the process of structuring dramatic activity so that the use of conventions can be seen as part of a dynamic process that enables participants to make, explore and communicate meaning through theatre form. In this sense, the conventions offer a pallet of ideas and ways of working in drama from which a wide range of exploratory, devised and text based drama work can be created.

The conventions are drawn from a wide range of sources including process drama, applied theatre as well as the work of key practitioners such as Brecht, Stanislavski, Boal and others.

The book is not an exhaustive guide to the practical study of theatre; rather, it identifies varieties of form that might be used or experienced as part of the more comprehensive art-process of communicating and interpreting meanings through theatre. The conventions and the examples are designed to support and enrich the study of drama in the curriculum and can be used as supplementary material for the Cambridge IGCSE and other syllabuses. The range of conventions corresponds to the Cambridge IGCSE syllabus and would easily transfer to a scheme of work supporting the full syllabus, as well as to other schemes of work including the study of dramatic texts.

The emphasis is on conventions that are often used in exploratory and rehearsal stages of dramatic inquiry and performance. However, many of the conventions can also be adapted for use in performance and this will depend on the experience and creativity of teachers, practitioners and the groups they work with. Theatre has no rules of course, and we hope that the fluid use of conventions across the making and performing of theatre will add fresh and new ideas for communicating theatre to audiences.

It is assumed that, as with all art forms, the experience of theatre is distinguished from real-life experience by the conscious application of form to meaning in order to engage both the intellect and the emotions in a representation of meaning. In theatre, meanings, social codes and interactions are represented, shaped and crafted through the conventions of dramatic activity. The same would hold true for all other art forms that use recognisable and conscious conventions of form in order to convey meanings. It is assumed that understanding the possibilities (and limitations) of form gives insight into the medium of theatre, and offers participants the possibility of operating greater control over the medium and its personal and social uses.

Definitions of theatre and dramatic convention

The definitions of theatre and dramatic convention presented below assume the following:

- that the term theatre does not describe a single form of activity, e.g. the performance of a playwright's work to an audience
- that theatre exists as a process for the interpretation of human behaviour and meanings as well as for their expression; it responds to a basic human need to symbolise the world through art forms
- that meaningful and personally useful theatre activity is the right and prerogative of all people, enabling all to maximise the culture of their ethnicity, class, gender, age or ability
- that a comprehensive study of theatre needs to go beyond a consideration of dramatic texts and the skills associated with acting
- that understanding theatre is an active process that enables a participant to build from subjective responses to theatre experiences towards the formation of valid critical judgements and generalisations about the nature and availability of theatre.

For the purposes of this book the following working definitions are used:

Theatre is the direct experience that is shared when people imagine and behave as if they were other than themselves in some other place at another time. This definition seeks to encompass all forms of creative imitative behaviour – from the loose and spontaneous imaginative *play* of young children (which becomes internalised, but still used in later life as a way of rehearsing conversations and events to come) through to the more formal experience of *the play* performed by actors for an audience.

Meanings in theatre are created for both spectator and participant through the actor's fictional and symbolic uses of human presence in time and space. These may be enhanced by the symbolic use of objects, light and sound. Dramatic convention describes the form that this relationship takes at different stages of the theatrical experience. Some theatre traditions and syllabuses distinguish methods, styles and genres from 'conventions', we have borrowed from these traditions but the essential quality of 'Structuring Drama Work' is that it uses the term 'convention' to describe different ways of structuring actors in time and space across a broad range of drama and theatre applications.

Conventions are indicators of the way in which *time*, *space* and *presence* can interact and be imaginatively shaped to create different kinds of meanings in theatre. Particular conventions will, therefore, emphasise different qualities in the theatrical possibilities of time, space and human presence. In terms of time, for instance, an improvisation will create a relationship that is very close to reality in the sense that time elapses at life-rate and the actor behaves and uses space naturalistically: in **still-image** time is arrested and frozen so that a period of time can be spent enquiring into a single moment represented in the tableau; in **mimed activity** the actor's use of space is often overtly symbolic, going beyond 'natural' gesture and uses of space in order to communicate specific meanings.

Part 1 of this book provides some of the conventions that make up the 'palette' that organisers1 and participants use in theatre; the application of the palette to create a picture requires those skills of sensitivity, perception and craft that develop through practical involvement and experimentation in theatre itself. Parts 2 and 3, therefore, introduce processes that may assist participants and organisers in exploring the applications of the palette of conventions.

---

[1] Throughout this book we use the term 'organiser' to describe those individuals who take responsibility for structuring the drama work of others. The term therefore encompasses applied theatre practitioners, teachers, directors, youth leaders and so on, as well as those participants working within self-initiating drama groups who take short-term responsibility for the group's experience at particular points in the process.

Part 1   A guide to dramatic conventions

Rationale

The definitions of theatre offered above have stressed a broad unity across a range of activities that have the imaginative and fictional use of time, space and presence as their common feature. Theatre is not seen as a narrow or exclusive set of culturally bound forms. The definitions are chosen in order to fix the book in contexts where theatre is being created by ordinary people and in recognition of the need to define a process in theatre that provides a continuity and development of experience across an age range that finds its first theatre experiences in play; to a generation that finds its satisfaction in a wide variety of contexts, including seeing and being in plays. These definitions influenced the selection of conventions in two important ways that, together, reflect the values of theatre and education held in this book:

- The conventions and the examples emphasise interactive forms of interchange, even fusion, of the roles of spectator and actor, rather than those conventions associated with performance where the roles of spectator and actor tend to be more clearly defined. *The conventions selected are mainly concerned with the process of theatre as a means of developing understanding about both human experience and theatre itself*. This may, or may not, later become translated and communicated through performance.
- The conventions have been chosen to emphasise theatre's traditional role as an educative form of entertainment that responds to a basic human need to interpret and express the world through symbolic form. The conventions recognise that theatre is not taught, rather that our own basic uses of theatre in play and other forms of imitative behaviour become refined and developed by experiencing increasingly complex relationships of convention and content. *The conventions selected, therefore, form a bridge between spontaneous and innate uses of theatre and the more poetic conventions of performance craft*. They are consciously associated with other familiar popular culture forms in order to stress the familiarity and pervasiveness of theatre.

Classification and criteria for selection

The conventions have been organised into groups that represent four varieties of dramatic action:

 Context-building action
Conventions that either 'set the scene', or add information to the context of the drama as it unfolds.

 Narrative action
Conventions that tend to emphasise the 'story' or 'what-happens-next' dimension of the drama.

 Poetic action
Conventions that emphasise or create the symbolic potential of the drama through highly selective use of language and gesture.

 Reflective action
Conventions that emphasise 'soliloquy' or 'inner-thinking' in the drama, or allow groups to review the drama from within the dramatic context.

This classification is not intended to be hierarchical or sequential. A convention achieves value through being appropriate to the moment for which it has been selected, and the dynamic nature of theatre requires shifts to and from different varieties of action as the experience unfolds.

The idea of a classification system is based on the notion that any such classification will be fluid in its boundaries and will serve as a means of making the entire list of conventions more manageable when choices about form need to be made. The handling of a convention in practice may result in a crossover of boundaries; a move from narrative action to poetic action, for instance.

The classification has been developed in response to certain basic needs required for participation, either as a spectator or as an actor, in dramatic activity:

- **Need for a clearly defined context**
  Theatre presents us with imagined situations in which a shared understanding of place, time, characters and other contextual information becomes crucial to the quality of involvement in the experience.

- **Need to nurture and create an interest in 'what happens next'**
  Theatre is defined as a narrative form, like story and film, in which curiosity about the storyline and a sense of imminent action act as motivation for those acting or spectating in the dramatic event.

- **Need to recognise and create a symbolic dimension to the work**
  Theatre provides a means of looking beyond the immediate story or plot through the symbols, ambiguities and imagery that are capable of crystallising, projecting and holding the essence of an experience.

- **Need to reflect on the meanings and themes that emerge through the experience**
  Theatre provides a 'mirror' in which actors and spectators can consider themselves and their relationship to others.

- **Need for choices to be made about the form of the work**
  Emphasis on participants gaining knowledge of the demands and uses of different conventions allows for a negotiated choice of conventions. *Psychologically, the group need to feel comfortable and protected enough to risk themselves in the convention. The organiser or facilitator often needs to negotiate a convention that creates a balance between the desire to motivate and inspire the group and the need to keep the activity controlled and manageable.*

Organisation of entries for the conventions

The entry for each convention is necessarily brief and practically orientated. An entry does not aim to represent a convention fully in its complexity. Indeed, an understanding of the particularity or essential qualities of a convention is seen as growing, in part, from the participants' active experimentation with form. It also develops through a shared analysis of the interaction between form and content that begins when the participants are provided with the opportunity and climate in which to articulate and make sense of their own felt responses to the use of a convention in practice.

The entry for each convention is arranged under the following headings:

- **Description**
  An explanation of how the convention is operated, and the different forms it might take. There will be many other variations of each convention that are not identified.

- **Cultural connections**
  The purpose of this section is to recognise and raise the status of theatre as a cultural resource that taps people's shared understanding of media/story conventions as well as conventions associated with their own immediate culture – that in turn reflects specific class, gender and racial variations and qualities. There is an emphasis on conventions that are borrowed from, or closely connect with, popular culture.

- **Learning opportunity**
  Each convention mediates and transforms meanings in a different way. For instance, meanings associated with family life are fundamentally different when expressed through dance conventions as opposed to monologue or soliloquy. This heading attempts to give a broad outline of the learning features highlighted by each convention in order to give some idea of what each represents as a form of learning.

- **Examples**
  Very brisk snapshots of conventions in practice that illustrate a convention being used for a particular purpose. The examples are not complete lessons or workshops; they are isolated moments taken from more extensive and coherent programmes.

Two of the major limitations of this section need to be stressed:

- Each convention described within the section appears isolated from others by the need to identify and separate conventions for the sake of clarity. In practice there is an integration of form in which conventions run into each other, or overlap, or merge into new composite conventions. An essential feature of theatre is that the dramatic experience develops and accumulates, so that responses to a convention used at one stage in the experience have to be taken within the context of the responses generated by the previous convention and the responses offered by the convention that follows. The possibility of creating relationships between conventions in order to develop ideas or to give an appropriate rhythm to the structure of a dramatic exercise – its own internal coherence – is seen as a central skill-area in theatre.

- The list of conventions that follows is not intended to impress or overwhelm in terms of quantity: *the real skill is not in making lists but in knowing which convention to select in order to establish appropriateness between:*
  (a) the needs and experience of the group
  (b) the content chosen for the drama
  (c) opportunities for learning.

A. Context-building action

Circle of life	Making maps/diagrams
Circular drama	Objects of character
Collective character	Role-on-the-wall
Collective drawing	Simulations
Commission	Soundtracking
Defining space	Still-image
Diaries, letters, journals, messages	Theory-building
First impressions	The iceberg
Games	The ripple
Guided tour	Unfinished materials

Uses

These conventions enable a group to create or engage with the dramatic context: the concrete particulars of the situation, characters or roles that will inform and drive the action. They are helpful when there is a need to:

- clarify the context through fixing time, place and people involved
- create atmosphere through use of space, light and sound
- draw attention to contextual constraints or opportunities
- find and make symbols and themes for the work
- check out possible different interpretations of the context held in the group.

Cultural origins

Life experience of building dens, designing rooms, arranging furniture; expectations created by different settings – dark woods, high-tech rooms, and so on. Conventions are drawn from theatre/film, e.g. **soundtracking** and **defining space** (set-building), and from psychotherapy, e.g. **games**, **simulations** and **still-image**.

Level of demand

Because the work is to do with setting up the context, rather than acting within it, there is little threat or personal risk involved. The work is indirect and involves groups contributing to a context that will be shared. *Commitment to dramatic action is gained through the small-group work and the sense of ownership generated, as well as through the interest created in seeing how the context might be used in the drama.*

Circle of life

Description	A large sheet of paper is divided into five sections with a circle in the centre of the page where the name and age of a character are written. The surrounding paper is then divided into four sections that will represent areas of that character's life and the people they interact with at those times. These sections are labelled: **Home**, **Family**, **Play** and **Day**.
	The heading **Home** indicates where the character normally lives, while **Family** indicates any immediate or extended family and may include estranged family members we might otherwise expect to find at home. **Play** indicates any type of social life and, finally, **Day** indicates the character's workplace, if appropriate, or otherwise encompasses their daily routine, for example if they are too young to work or are unemployed. These headings are hopefully as value-free as possible so that groups can determine for themselves the specifics of the entries to be made. The group then brainstorms ideas about the character and these ideas are entered into the appropriate section.
	The group is then subdivided into four smaller groups, each of which takes a different section and creates a short dialogue between the central character and one other character selected from their chosen section of the diagram. These encounters are initially based on the previous collective agreements.
Cultural connections	Significant others; those whose lives influence our own; Google Plus – the organisation of one's circles; WhatsApp – groups and their representation of different aspects of one's life; Pinterest – people represent their areas of interest and activities.
Learning opportunities	Negotiation and selection of content; sequencing of ideas; building a complex character from minimal clues; extrapolating and analysing human behaviour on the basis of influences and social relationships.

Example

1   As the starting point for an exploratory drama the group are shown the following brief performance with the organiser in the role as Sunita.

> My name is Sunita. I am fourteen. That is my mother. (She points to another actor standing with her back to Sunita (**prepared roles**).) She is in the kitchen washing the dishes. In the sitting room I can see her bag lying open on a chair. This is my only chance of being saved. My little brother and father are outside playing football. The room is empty. I hate what I must do. I love my mother but I have no choice. I must have that money.

The organiser now improvises with the mother character using whatever distractions/excuses/tactics necessary to take the money. The mother's prepared role has been briefed so that she can make further character information available to the group by, for example, calling upstairs for both her husband and son by name during this encounter. As she leaves Sunita again narrates:

> I can't believe I've done it. I hate myself for what I've done. Perhaps I can put it back before she notices … no, too late. I can hear my father coming downstairs. That's it. No turning back. I've done it now. At least I'll be safe.

The organiser comes out of the role and facilitates a discussion on what the group have learnt from what they have seen and the group come up with what is for them the main question of the drama: what does Sunita mean by 'At least I'll be safe'?

Figure 1 represents the preliminary decision-making following these inputs with information gleaned from both Sunita and her mother, and this becomes the basis for the initial, small-group improvisations that follow. New information can be added as it is clarified.

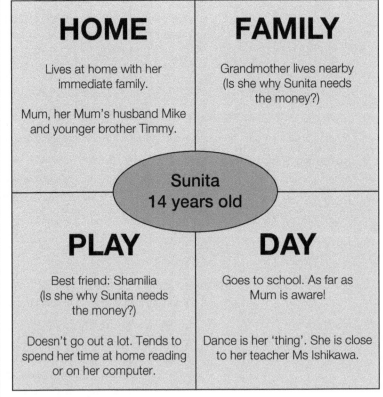

Figure 1   The group's entries about Sunita

Circular drama

Description	This convention is essentially a more manageable form of **teacher-in-role** for the less experienced and less confident. The group is organised into a series of subgroups, each of which has a specific relationship with a central character. The group decide on their individual roles and the physical location of their group. The organiser takes on the role of the central character and enters the small-group action in random sequence, improvising briefly with each group before moving on. The remaining groups are audience during this activity.
Cultural connections	Scenes in any form of drama that reveal a central character's story or journey and relationships with other characters; an online MMORPGs profile gaming history; YouTube Profiles and their comment history and subscription list.
Learning opportunities	Provides the opportunity to see the different ways in which a character reacts in a variety of public and private contexts; deepens understanding of choices to be made; fun.

Example

1 Participants are exploring *The Wise Old Woman* (Prentice Hall & IBD, 1994), a story by Yoshiko Uchida involving the central dilemma of a young farmer, living in a village ruled by a cruel lord, who is ordered by the lord to take his elderly mother (the Wise Old Woman of the story) and leave her to die on a mountainside because she is too old. Four groups are established as follows:

Old Woman's friends – in the tea-house
Market traders – in the marketplace
Farmer's friends – in the inn
Young children of the village – in a play area.

The time is the evening of the day before the Wise Old Woman is due to be taken away. The organiser, in role as the Wise Old Woman, improvises with each of the groups, challenging their thinking. So if the group feel that she should not submit, then she stresses duty and tradition. If, however, the group feel she must do what she is told, then she stresses her love of life and the favours she has previously done for those in the group, e.g. all those sweets she has given to the young children when she's seen them around the village!

Collective character

Description	A character is improvised by a group, any one of whom can speak as that character. Alternatively, an individual opts to take on the role and the remainder of the group whisper advice and offer lines of dialogue to be spoken by the volunteer. In this way a large group can be involved in the creation of a dialogue with, for instance, subgroups taking on responsibility for each of the characters involved. In order to encourage contributions there need not be conformity in the early responses and different attitudes can initially be given expression. However, in the long term decisions will need to be made on the truthfulness of a character's responses in order to achieve a unified, collective representation.
Cultural connections	Team games; **rituals** and **ceremonies**; Facerig and other digital embodiment software; Xbox Kinect and shared avatar manipulation.
Learning opportunities	Requires participants to work sensitively and collectively; sharing a role through alternative portrayals; tests out character responses in action; helps provide a more complex character for further exploration.

Examples

1 In a play-building drama based on an advert in a corner shop placed by a woman selling her wedding dress, wedding and engagement rings, small groups have built up a series of scenes to show why the marriage might have gone wrong. At the end of the drama a dialogue is held between the 'woman who sells the dress' (the voice of experience) and 'the woman who comes to buy the dress' (the voice of innocence). Two volunteers silently represent the women while the rest of the group decide which 'woman' they wish to speak for and place themselves behind the appropriate role.

2 In a drama based on Angela Carter's re-telling of the Little Red Riding Hood story (*The Bloody Chamber and Other Stories*), the group take on the collective role of Little Red Riding Hood in order to work with the **teacher in role** as the mother. Individuals can ask any questions of the mother in order to elicit information about the context and setting of the story.

Elaboration

In this variation of a basic convention called 'Echoes', two volunteers, each supported by other group members, play characters involved in a dialogue. These individuals provide this dialogue through short sentences and phrases, which are echoed by the subgroups supporting them.

Collective drawing

Description	Working either as one group or in small groups participants make a collective image to represent a place or people in the drama. The image then becomes a concrete reference for ideas that are being discussed, or that are half-perceived.
Cultural connections	Illustrations; media imagery; photos of urban/rural landscapes; portraits; use of drawing for own purposes; comics; cartoons; posters; postcards; online collaborative drawing software such as Adobe Photoshop Touch, Brushes 3, or Sketchbook Pro.
Learning opportunities	Giving form to imagined places and faces; negotiating a common response in relation to appearances; researching authenticity in drawings of different cultures or historical periods; division of labour in performing the task.

Examples

1　A group of 'pioneers' are planning to go West on a wagon train. In order to establish their motives for undertaking such an epic journey, and how it fits with their past, the group prepare two **collective drawings** for display – one represents the place they have migrated from, with clues as to what made them leave; the second represents their imaginings of their destination.

2　A group working on 'Mining' have just read Sid Chaplin's *Hands* (Penguin English Project 'Danger', Ward Lock, 1977). The story describes an accident in which the narrator's father is crushed by a rockfall, so that his hands are all that is left exposed. In the role of book illustrators, groups work with charcoal and chalk to make images depicting the end of the story.

3　A group are working with Antony Browne's *Into the Forest* (Walker Books, 2004) in which a young boy is woken by a terrible sound in the night and in the morning finds his father has gone from home. His mother sends him into the forest to take a cake to his grandmother, who is unwell. As the boy goes through the forest he meets various fairy-tale characters, who try to take his grandmother's cake. Eventually he discovers that his father has not disappeared but has instead gone to look after his grandmother.

　　The group makes a **collective drawing** of the forest on a long roll of paper. They work in detail and consider different zones of the forest. When they are finished, a volunteer walks through the forest while the rest of the group provide a **soundscape** of his journey. The forest is used as a set during the drama that follows and finally the boy and his father return home, while the group provide a second **soundscape** – how have the boy's perceptions of the forest changed?

Commission

Description	This convention is a means of setting a collective task with clear expectations and a real-world purpose. The task itself may be an opportunity to 'experience' and 'make use' of disciplinary knowledge, abstract, ethical and moral thinking and social co-discovery. There is also a tension that will make the task more complex and ethically difficult. The **commission** may be complex and require trans-disciplinary teams and adequate time. The **commission** is usually given to a group who are then encouraged to become an autonomous enterprise and to use their collective resources to create something that has a real-world connection. But they must also accept the 'mantle' of their enterprise. They must approach the task and each other according to their given occupation and task orientation rather than as themselves.
Cultural connections	Curating exhibitions; editing collections or preparing evidence, organising conferences or building digital platforms; working as designers; renovating the past; working as artists.
Learning opportunities	**Commissions** require participants to work together and work to real-world specifications and expectations. The playfulness of the imagined task and roles encourages participants to look for creative possibilities, vary their approach, find an effective consensus, use dialogue to build and communicate ideas, and enjoy responding to obstacles and challenges.

Examples

1   In an 'Executive Education' course looking at qualities of leadership in a crisis, the participants are looking at Creon in Sophocles *Antigone* through the lens of the following **commission**:

You are consultants representing a variety of organisations that are interested in new, high-risk markets. Recently, you helped clients assess the commercial potential of Tripoli, Damascus and Baghdad.

Thebes is one of these high-risk markets and you can discern both the city's risks and potential. You can see the city is in a state of chaos, but you can also discern its resources and possibilities. You are about to meet the city's new ruler who is responsible for reinstating order so that the city starts functioning as a safe and thriving market. What needs to happen in Thebes in order to achieve its potential?

Working in teams, you are asked to do the following:

Decide on the sector you represent – pharmaceutical, health, telecommunications, energy, etc. – and discuss the ethical and commercial considerations of entering the market of Thebes. What conditions will you set as a prerequisite before you invest? What improvements need to be made? Identify three conditions or improvements that would need to be met for Thebes to become a new market. Be prepared to discuss the key leadership qualities that will bring Thebes back from the brink of disaster. What kind of leadership would you expect in such a situation?

Group discussions are interrupted by a summons to attend a meeting with Creon, the king of Thebes (organiser in role). The king makes a chilling speech in which he explains that he must act ruthlessly and decisively to stamp out the threat of civil war. In his speech, the king clearly sets out his leadership style. Subsequently, he invites questions from the group. This gives participants the opportunity to ascertain whether Creon represents the leadership style that they see fit for Thebes, in order to invest in the city.

Finally, while the participants are with Creon, they learn of the punishment he intends for his niece Antigone for disobeying his direct orders. The group are left to answer the following questions:

- What do you think Creon should do in this situation?
- What would you advise Creon to do?
- Is Creon the right leader for this situation?
- Would you recommend investing in Thebes?

2 In an MBA module 'Leadership and the Art of Judgement' students are given the following **commission** to deepen their understanding of Shakespeare's *King Lear* and to develop team and interactive skills.

The brief is as follows: 'Your commission is to re-create an art gallery exhibition based on the representation of **King Lear** in art. The exhibition package has arrived with a set of paintings and quotations from the play. Lear's speech (below) is to be at the heart of the exhibition, but the curator has not sent any other instructions on how the paintings and texts should be displayed and in what sequence. **You will have to use your own creativity and judgment to recreate the exhibition in the space allocated to you and using the materials provided.'**

Meantime we shall express our darker purpose.
Give me the map there. Know that we have divided
In three our kingdom. and 'tis our fast intent
To shake all cares and business from our age,
Conferring them on younger strengths while we
Unburdened crawl toward death.
(Act 1, Scene 1)

Defining space

Description	Any available material and furniture is used to 'accurately' represent the place where a drama is happening; or to represent the physical scale of something in the drama; or to fix the position and proximity of rooms, houses, places where events have taken place.
Cultural connections	Sets used in media drama; film locations; rearranging furniture at home; imaginative use of adventure playgrounds (and other places where children and young people play or socialise); green screening, using pre-set backgrounds on photo-apps such as Photo Booth and Framey; virtual reality gameplay: Oculus Rift and Project Morpheus.
Learning opportunities	Using available resources imaginatively; negotiating the way a place should look; representing meanings spatially; encouraging belief in the fiction by working to elaborate it; reflecting on relationships between context and action.

Examples

1   As a way in to considering the effect of imprisonment on adult offenders, groups working as architects are asked to build cells using available materials, so that the dimensions and what is inside the cell can be seen. The 'cells' are compared and discussed, and then compared against the dimensions of an actual cell and against regulations covering what is allowed inside.

2   The group are at an inquiry into the murder of a young film star on a film set. The group reconstruct the film set using available materials, and position the body as it would have looked when it was first discovered.

Diaries, letters, journals, messages

Description	These texts are written in or out of role as a means of reflecting on experience; or are introduced into the drama by the organiser as a new tension, or as evidence; or they are used as a means of reviewing work or building up a cumulative account of a long sequence of work.
Cultural connections	Personal diaries; books and stories written in journal or diary form; answerphone messages; telegrams; letters from relatives and friends; letters to the press; secret codes; cryptic messages; spy stories; travelogues; Facebook Personal Messages; Facebook Secret Groups; Online Clans and Teams; hacking groups such as Anonymous publicly posting declarations.
Learning opportunities	Selecting content; adopting appropriate registers and vocabulary; writing from alternative viewpoints; arousing curiosity with unexpected or cryptic messages; providing a form for reflection; motivating purposes for writing; providing imagined audiences for writing.

Examples

1   Playing with the traditional story of Goldilocks and the Three Bears, group members write:

   (a) Goldilocks' letter of apology to the bears
   (b) Baby Bear's letter to his best friend describing his experiences
   (c) Newspaper articles by reporters for 'The Quadruped Times' and the 'Daily People'
   (d) Police reports and witness statements
   (e) Estimates for furniture repair from the Guild of Furniture Makers.

2   In constructing a context for a murder inquiry, a group work on providing some of the clues found at the scene of the crime, e.g. **still-images** representing photos found in the victim's bag. It is decided that the victim was clutching the fragments of a letter when found. In sub-groups each small group makes two fragments with a word on each; these are then arranged on a grid to see if they give a clue to what the original message might have been.

First impressions

Description	Group members use a pie chart split into three sections, headed **Know**, **Want to Know** and **Guess** (as in Figure 2), as a way of recording their initial understandings and feelings concerning a character and determining the questions they intend to pursue in the course of their future drama work. As the group develop their understandings of the character, they can return to the outline and shift entries from one section to another or change any aspect of their original choices and decisions they made.
	As with all paper conventions, this convention is portable and can be moved for use in any space. At the same time it can also be used as an aid to reflection at the end of a session and to refocus on the work at the start of the next.

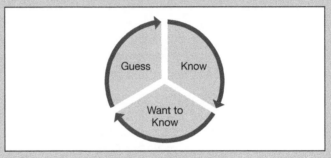

Figure 2   Understandings of a character

Cultural connections	Reading and understanding the clues people offer us about themselves, e.g. word clues; making sense of the behaviour of others; predicting the behaviour of others.
Learning opportunities	Extrapolation from reflective analysis of a character and initial perceptions of the character's behaviour; encourages speculation and the interpretation of clues and actions; encourages belief in the fiction through making demands on the participants to suspend disbelief and imagine future possibilities; offers participants influence over the character's development.

Example

1   This example begins with a simple, rehearsed scene – although other stimuli might also be used - in which the organiser takes on the role of a character we shall initially identify as B.

Scene: a table, with a couple of chairs – could be any location in a house. B enters the room, carrying her bag and wearing a colourful hat. She is obviously anxious, and has something on her mind. She paces up and down the room. Finally she sits and opens the bag and takes out a photograph. She then appears to look lovingly at the photo and finally kisses it. She then returns to her original mood and shuffles around in her chair, looking at her watch. It is obvious she is concerned about the time. She then stands up calls out: 'Mum, Mum ...' but there is no answer. She then picks up her bag, appears to make a decision and leaves the room.

A possible but not the only interpretation of this scene would be that B represents a young adult who has been refused permission to go out with her friend by a parent or carer. However, B makes a decision for herself and goes out regardless.

Following this scene the group are asked to share their initial feelings and responses to what they have just seen. Then they are invited to look inside the character's bag (**objects of character**) and take out and discuss the significance of any of the items that it contains, before returning them exactly as they found them.

The group are then introduced to the **first impressions** diagram. The figure represents the character in the scene and the group should now agree on a name for that character.

The scene is then shown again and the group are asked to decide on:

- anything they think they know about the character
- what they would infer or guess about the character from their behaviour
- what they would like to know about the character.

These ideas are now held and may be returned to at any future point for further discussion, during which further ideas may be added or existing views clarified as the drama unfolds.

Games

Description	Games are used to establish trust or confidence, or to establish rules; games can simplify a complex experience; games are put into the context of drama rather than played for their own sake.
Cultural connections	Street games; quiz shows; card and board games; team games; psychological games; computer games; mobile games; online console games; educational games; tests of skill, strength, endurance.
Learning opportunities	Highly controlled – players must submit to rules; enjoyable, fun activity; highlights tensions in social situations; useful for breaking the ice, reveals game structures in life situations – blocking, hiding, deceiving, and so on.

Example

1   A devising ensemble are working on the theme of 'soldiering', using a **montage** of historical and contemporary poetry, literature and factual materials. They play the following games to explore the idea of comradeship and the individual's conditioning by army life.

Bomb and shield: Participants walk the space. Each participant picks on another, who becomes their personal 'bomb'. They must keep as far as possible from the 'bomb'. Then each participant chooses another as their personal 'shield'. Now each participant must move around the space so that their 'shield' is always between them and their bomb.

Huggies: Huggies is an informal way of quickly making groups of varied sizes. The group walk around the space and the organiser calls out 'Huggies', followed by an action and a number. The group must then split into groups of the required size and create an image that mirrors the action – for example as comrades coming home from war; as comrades going to war; at a service for the fallen.

Stop, go, jump, clap: Participants walk around the space and respond to orders to 'stop', 'go', 'jump', 'clap'. Then the orders are reversed so that stop = go, go = stop, clap = jump and jump = clap.

1, 2, 3: In pairs, first speaker says 1, next person 2, first person 3, next person 2, and so on. Then the number 1 is replaced by a clap; then 2 becomes a stamp; then 3 is a finger click. So the sequence 1, 2, 3 becomes a 1, 2, 3 then clap, 2, 3 then clap, stomp, finally 3 becomes clap, stomp, click. Both this and the previous game emphasise following orders even when they are uncertain, routines, drills and so on.

Protect the fallen: Participants are numbered 1 to 5 and then walk around the space. When the organiser calls out a number, all those with that number 'faint' and the others must protect them and make sure they do not fall to the floor. After a while the 'fallen' must be taken off the 'battlefield' until none are left.

Guided tour

Description	A form of **narration** through which the group are provided with a detailed picture of the environment in which the drama is due to take place. This convention involves talking the group through the drama's setting – building-based, natural, fantastic and so on – using a highly descriptive commentary that both places and details the key features of that location.
Cultural connections	Tours of museums, stately homes and tourist locations; geolocation-based apps and games; FourSquare; Geoguessr; QONQR; guided tours on Google Maps and other mapping software.
Learning opportunities	Giving form to imagined places and locations; encouraging collective belief in the fiction; facilitating a common response.

Examples

1 Participants in role as ambassadors from Athens have come to Crete to intercede with King Minos over his sacrifice of Athenian youths to the Minotaur. They are met by the organiser in role as Daedalus, the architect of the Labyrinth. Daedalus takes the ambassadors on a **guided tour** of King Minos' palace and even a short way into the Labyrinth, before showing them to a place of rest prior to a meeting with the king.

2 When Badger dies, the other animals are at first inconsolable, but gradually, one by one, they remember the special gifts that Badger taught them, the memories of which they will treasure always. As an introduction to Susan Varley's picture storybook *Badger's Parting Gifts* (Andersen, 2013) a group are asked to draw furniture for Badger's home and are then taken on a **guided tour** to see the furniture in situ, which has remained untouched since Badger died.

3 A group are exploring the importance of Elsinore as a setting for the story of William Shakespeare's *Hamlet*. Half of the group look at an atmospheric drawing of the inside of a castle and half at the outside battlements and towers. The interior group prepare to give a **guided tour** in role as old and established servants to newly arrived servants, and the exterior group as old soldiers to new recruits into the army. The theme for the servants' tour is 'Don't get lost!', and for the soldiers it is 'The Norwegians are coming'. Each participant finds a partner in the other group and they take it in turns to close their eyes and be led through the space on a **guided tour**. Then they walk back on their own, with eyes closed, to the spot where the experience of the 'tour' was most powerful for them. The organiser then **thought-tracks** each participant and asks what they can see in their mind's eye.

Making maps/diagrams

Description	**Making maps/diagrams** is used as part of a drama in order to reflect on experience, e.g. obstacles to be overcome, distance to be travelled; or to aid problem-solving, e.g. 'what's the best way of getting into the fortress?'; or after the drama, as a means of reviewing the work; or are introduced by the organiser as a stimulus.
Cultural connections	Maps – old and new; making things from instructions/diagrams; giving/receiving directions; treasure/secret maps; map/diagram conventions in thriller/journey stories; map-work in humanities; geocaching; creating own journeys in digital mapping software such as Google Maps; adding to OpenStreetMap through GPS mapping of an area.
Learning opportunities	Getting detail/layout/scale of maps accurate and comprehensible; representing problems diagrammatically; deciphering/interpreting maps and symbols; reflecting on what maps/diagrams tell us about the experience they represent.

Examples

1 An issue-based drama exploring the problems and long-term effects of land mines is based on maps made by the group of a valley, somewhere in Central Europe. The valley is divided into three sections and groups are asked to imagine and then map what might be in their section: farms, natural resources, roads, paths, houses, and so on. They are also asked to map a 'journey of necessity' and a 'journey of pleasure'. This activity helps the group to imagine themselves as a peasant farming community with its traditions and sense of place. Following an enforced evacuation the peasants are shown the maps again, in a briefing from the UN, before returning home. The location of known minefields has been added to the map – what dangers/changes will this mean for the peasant farmers?

2 A group in role as bank robbers gain access to the blueprints of a high-security bank to help them plan their robbery. They represent their route on a transparency that can be laid over the blueprint so that they can explain to others the advantages and disadvantages of their plan.

Objects of character

Description	This convention allows for both the creation and/or the fleshing out of a character through consideration of a carefully chosen assemblage of personal belongings. The organiser's selection of the objects should give clues about the character of their owner. The items can be 'found' as a means of introducing a character or the character's setting. The role can be encountered at any point before or after their possessions have been made available to the group and their behaviour may well be at variance with, and even contradictory to, the group's particular interpretation. In this way, the character's private property forms a subtext to their words and actions.
	Items can be extremely varied but need to have the potential to raise questions for the group – keys, tickets, postcards, photographs, letters, costume and so on. The group have the opportunity, in the no-penalty zone of the drama, to handle intimate and private objects and can attempt to interpret these items in terms of possible character traits.
	Alternatively, the group can be asked to 'gift' objects, talents, understanding and so on, to a central character within the drama (see **gifting**). These gifts can be either real items or drawn/written on paper. Here the choice of 'objects' is the group's, but their decisions must be based on a consideration of the appropriateness of the objects to the character in question.
Cultural connections	Personal effects; inventories; wills; common device in realist drama; wearable/portable technology; choice of apps; how people comment and interact through social media on important occasions; the marking of special times or occasions: birthdays, name days, feasts, prize-giving.
Learning opportunities	Deconstructing/interpreting information; divining a character's personality from clothing or personal artefacts; weighing interpretation against perceived behaviour. Encourages belief in the fiction by making an immediate intellectual and emotional demand on each group member; stimulates consideration of the demands and tensions presented by a future situation; offers participants an element of investment in and influence over the character's imminent action.

Examples

1 A short scene is presented to the group in which they witness a young woman waiting, getting progressively more agitated, calling for her mother without response and leaving in haste. The group is invited to consider what they can learn about the young woman from the contents of her handbag, which she has forgotten in her anxiety to be gone.

2 Participants are in role as the workers in a factory. In order to avoid a stereotypical, Victorian-style factory owner, the character is created through the careful selection of items both on show and out of sight in the drawers of his/her office desk.

3 The organiser asks the group to establish a character from a bundle of clothes and belongings that have been found on a cliff. The bundle includes an old jacket, baggy trousers, muddy rag bandages, a length of string, a knife, a woollen cap, a bundle of newspapers, a tobacco tin, a rag doll, a tripod and cooking tin. From these clues the group create the role of Albert, a derelict traveller.

They go on to discuss what each object reveals about the man who owns them. The subsequent drama is to do with discovering what might have happened to Albert.

Role-on-the-wall

Description	An important role is represented as an outline of a human figure 'on the wall'; information is read or added as the drama progresses. Individuals may take turns to adopt the role in improvisations, so that it becomes a collective representation.
Cultural connections	Portraits; posters; characters in books, films, TV; memes; GIFs; legendary figures; cartoons; personal records and files; imitating well-known figures.
Learning opportunities	Distanced, reflective way of building a deep understanding of a role; building a complex character from scratch; sharing a role through alternative portrayals; strong form for exploring human characteristics and behaviour.

Examples

1   As a means of exploring the experience of old age, the group are shown a highly selective, atmospheric, life-size charcoal and chalk drawing of a senior with a series of factual statements about his life. The drawings and statements contain a rich variety of signs about the man's likely attitudes to old age. The group enter information onto the **role-on-the-wall** outline, indicating that they are guessing by recording their observations around the figure.

   Then the group recreate the man's life in the manner of a photograph album, and as they refine their guesswork through working on the character, they transfer 'known' information into the outline itself.

2   In a drama looking at the story of an uncooperative teenager, the organiser draws a rough outline of a human figure. As a starting point, the group record a series of statements made about the figure by a parent, a teacher, a psychologist and a friend; these are written around the outline of the figure. As the work progresses, new understandings about the teenager are written inside the figure as an aid to reflection and to record the growing complexity of the characterisation.

3   Beginning a devising process to create a piece for performance, each actor completes an outline of a human figure. Inside the outline they list what experiences, skills, attitudes and feelings they bring to the process. Around the outline they list what questions they have and the answers they seek through the work.

4   Actors collecting seniors' stories for a **reminiscence theatre** project create a **role-on-the-wall** for each individual they interview. Inside the outline they record recollections from the past and around the outline they include seniors' feelings about the present and their hopes for the future.

Simulations

Description	Life events are simulated in such a way as to emphasise management of resources, decision-taking, problem-solving, institutional management. A time limit is often set for 'players', so that there is a game tension. **Simulations** may be a commercially produced pack including role cards, pretend money and other pieces, or a pack produced by one group for another.
Cultural connections	War games; Dungeons and Dragons; computer games; strategy games; guild management within MMORPGs; turn-based competitive online games; Settlers of Catan; card-based trading games: Magic: the Gathering; Monopoly; Risk; and so on.
Learning opportunities	Problems presented within contexts that require group decision-making and problem-solving; structured but encourages identification with the problem; rules and prepared materials make it possible for complex interactions between supply and demand, time and personnel to be examined.

Examples

1   As part of a project looking at development and aid strategies, participants decide between projects submitted by other groups. They have a fixed budget to allocate and use their own criteria for selection. The exercise involves interviewing proposers and potential beneficiaries of the schemes, and encourages participants to look for a balance between cost and long-term effect.

2   Research for a documentary drama on homelessness involves participants in a simulation in which they have a set number of places to distribute among a group who present themselves as homeless. The players use local government criteria in order to decide who gets the shelter. The drama goes on to explore the consequences for those getting shelter and those who are left homeless.

Soundtracking

Description	Realistic or stylised sounds accompany action, or describe an environment. Dialogue is devised to fit a given piece of action. Sound from one situation is 'dubbed' onto another. Voices or instruments are used to create a mood or paint a picture.
Cultural connections	Sound effects on film and TV; street sounds; pop videos; GarageBand; SonicFire; music on film and TV; noises that disturb – being followed, breaking glass, and so on.
Learning opportunities	Matching sound to action; using sound poetically and expressively to convey mood and a sense of place; exploring dissonance between soundtrack and images; encouraging confidence in use of voice as a wide-ranging instrument.

Examples

1   A group is working on the 'Great Fire of London'. As museum curators they reconstruct Pudding Lane, the fire's starting point, using blocks, chairs and tables. They represent waxworks in the reconstruction, showing the different trades, home and street activities of the time. An imaginary switch is activated that starts a soundtrack of the sounds of the street. The sound starts at one end of the lane and travels down, adding new sounds as it goes. Later, noises illustrative of the fire and people fleeing from it move down the lane in much the same way.

2   A group have worked from a map of an inner-city area to create its pictorial representation. In the centre of this picture is a large park or open space with floral displays and mature trees and in which there is also a children's playground. Standing immediately adjacent to the playground is a community hall. Each group member has chosen one of the houses around the park as their own and has decided on their daily schedule.

'Yesterday' these people arrived home to find circular letters from a property developer telling them that the park is scheduled for redevelopment and inviting them to a meeting at 8.00 a.m. in the community hall. The group create a rehearsed soundtrack of the city awakening to start another new day using recorded and live sound, and at selected points open their front doors, greet their neighbours and head for the meeting.

Still-image

Description	Groups devise an image using their own bodies to crystallise a moment, idea or theme; or an individual acts as sculptor to a group. Contrasting images are made to represent actual/ideal, dream/nightmare versions.
Cultural connections	Book illustrations; freeze-frame/pause on a digital player; photographs; portraits; advertisements; sculptures; waxworks; posters; record sleeves; murals; selfies; Snapchat; memes; TwitchTV; screenshots.
Learning opportunities	Highly selective way of crystallising meaning into concrete images, a very economical and controlled form of expression as well as a sign to be interpreted or read by observers; groups are able to represent more than they would be able to communicate through words alone; a useful way of representing 'tricky' content such as fights; simplifies complex content into easily managed and understandable form; requires reflection and analysis in the making and observing of images.

Examples

1   The group are working on 'The Identification' by Roger McGough. In the poem a father is identifying the body of his teenage son and discovers that his son had a secret that the father either knew nothing about, or chose to deny. Groups take responsibility for making one of the following **still-images**, which are designed to reveal the two sides of the boy's personality:

   Stephen as his father would like to remember him
   Stephen as his friends do remember him
   Stephen as his grandma would like to remember him
   Stephen as his teachers do remember him.

2   A group are exploring the theme of 'first love', based on Andrez Voznenzky's poem 'First Frost'. The central image in the poem is of a young woman crying in a telephone box, experiencing the 'first ice of telephone phrases' (*Wordlife*, Thomas Nelson, 1988). The group divides into sub-groups, each of which makes two contrasting **still-images** of a moment that the couple might have shared (at a party/dance, walking in the park). The images show the different ways that the two people remember the same moment. The sub-groups work on melting/morphing from one image to the other. Each sub-group shares their two images with the other groups and those watching, then decide on which point in the transition from one image to the other is the point of greatest ambiguity, that is the point between the two selective memories of the same event.

The iceberg

Description

The image of an iceberg (Figure 3) is drawn on a large sheet of paper with the sea level marked in on the basis that 9/10ths of the main body of the iceberg is below water level. The outline is then used to collect together group observations concerning a character's personality and behaviour. Above the waterline the group record those personality traits that they imagine are immediately observable, while below the waterline they list those aspects of the character's make-up that they feel are likely to be kept private or hidden.

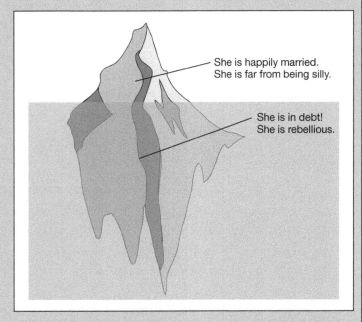

She is happily married.
She is far from being silly.

She is in debt!
She is rebellious.

Figure 3   Observing a character's public and private personality traits

Cultural connections

The difference between appearance and reality, the public and the private; Shakespeare/Macbeth: Duncan 'There's no art/To find the mind's construction in the face'; presenting one's best face to the world; avatars and internet gaming.

Learning opportunities

Reflection and analysis of character, and the relationships between context and action; deconstructing/interpreting information; concretising and holding information.

Example

1 At the end of Act 1 of Henrik Ibsen's *A Doll's House* (Cambridge University Press, 1995) the group are asked to use **the iceberg** to record their initial observations of Nora Helmer. They list them as follows:

Above the waterline

- She is generous – she tips.
- She is happily married to Torvald and seems basically content.
- He speaks to her in a patronising way, but she doesn't seem to mind. He calls her a 'featherbrain', 'Miss Sweet-tooth'.
- She is not just a 'silly girl', as Torvald calls her.
- She is determined and has ambition.
- She loves her children but fears she will corrupt them.
- She has a non-conformist streak.

Below the waterline (but near the surface)

- She has a secret debt that she is only able to tell Christine about.
- She lies.
- She is courageous but probably doesn't show it in everyday life.
- She is becoming aware that her life is at odds with her real personality.
- She is prepared to defy Torvald but as yet only in minor ways – by eating macaroons and then lying to him about it.
- She swears.
- She is ripe for rebellion.

As the play unfolds, **the iceberg** is used at further intervals to record the group's changing analysis, impressions and observations.

The ripple

Description	The characters involved in an unresolved and problematic event are sculpted in an image representing a frozen, introductory moment chosen to open the encounter. The image is brought to life slowly with each character in the image asked to make only one movement and one linked sound (language-based or pure sound as appropriate) in turn. The group decide the running order of this sequence, so that a group of three actors (A, B and C) might 'ripple' clockwise or anticlockwise, or even start with the character represented by B.
	The choice obviously depends on an assessment of the situation being rippled (for example, where the power lies within the grouping). When the sequence through the image is felt to generate a 'truthful' feeling for the moment represented, a second ripple can be overlaid on the first, and so on. At the point at which the group 'feel' the unfolding image is grounded in a moment of reality, **the ripple** can be released into full improvisation. Once created, **the ripple** gives a key, which provides easy access to return to and rework starting points as often as required.
Cultural connections	Waves; pebbles thrown into ponds; cogs in a machine; turn-based gaming; sharing on Facebook, trending.
Learning opportunities	Analysing significance of context and character relation as the springboard into action; encouraging a belief in the fiction by working to unlock it; physical and vocal control.

Examples

1   As part of a project exploring racism, participants take the following extract from Toni Morrison's novel *Sula* (Vintage, 1998) and 'ripple' the moment of contact between the girls and their tormentors, until such time as they are confident of its truthfulness. The group then use **Forum-theatre** to explore possible outcomes.

> Four white boys in their early teens, sons of some newly arrived Irish people, occasionally entertained themselves in the afternoon by harassing black schoolchildren. With shoes that pinched and woolen knickers that made red rings on their calves, they had come to this valley with their parents believing as they did that it was a promised land—green and shimmering with welcome. What they found was a strange accent, a pervasive fear of their religion and firm resistance to their attempts to find work. With one exception the older

residents of Medallion scorned them. The one exception was the black community. Although some of the Negroes had been in Medallion before the Civil War (the town didn't even have a name then), if they had any hatred for these newcomers it didn't matter because it didn't show. As a matter of fact, baiting them was the one activity that the white Protestant residents concurred in. In part their place in this world was secured only when they echoed the old residents' attitude towards blacks.

These particular boys caught Nel once, and pushed her from hand to hand until they grew tired of the frightened helpless face. Because of that incident, Nel's route home from school became elaborate. She, and then Sula, managed to duck them for weeks until a chilly day in November when Sula said, 'Let's us go on home the shortest way.'

Nel blinked, but acquiesced. They walked up the street until they got to the bend of Carpenter's Road where the boys lounged on a disused well. Spotting their prey, the boys sauntered forward as though there were nothing in the world on their minds but the gray sky. Hardly able to control their grins, they stood like a gate blocking the path.

2 In a drama exploring themes of migration, a devising ensemble represent men on the deck of a ship about to depart and the women and children standing on the dock to say their last farewells. The actors begin in a neutral position and are asked to ripple into character from one end of the line to the other and when all are in character they begin to whisper across the space of water between them what they want to say to their loved ones before the boat pulls away.

Theory-building

Description	**Theory-building** is an activity that requires the organiser to prepare, in advance, a series of laminated images and/or fragments of text: 8–10 are enough. Each laminate should address some aspect of the session's subject matter either directly or tangentially. It is important that the information does not lead participants in too specific a direction, but it must also be appropriate for their levels of knowledge and ability. The exercise is for groups of 8 to 30 people. The organiser divides the larger group into several appropriately sized smaller groups. The groups are then provided with a set of identical laminates. Each group is required to create a 'theory' from the materials and represent this as a pattern on the floor of the space. The organiser should be ready to step in at various moments to clarify, for example, what the images represent and from where the quotations are taken. When each group is ready, they invite another group over and share their 'theory'. The leader tries to remain detached so that groups have to take responsibility for and ownership of the task. Next they return to their guest group's space and hear and see that group's theory. Then the whole group discuss the similarities and differences in their **theory-building. Theory-building** is a good beginning exercise to a drama that allows participants to explore themes and ideas that will be important to the drama that follows.
Cultural connections	Experimentation; problem-solving; teamwork; curating exhibitions; editing.
Learning opportunities	Participants are required to engage by the nature of the activity. It both promotes collective action and encourages a sense of individual responsibility. It deepens understanding of the subject matter and provides a platform for later, more detailed material. It demonstrates that creativity is about discovering new possibilities. Even though all groups have the same materials, they will come up with different theories.

Examples

1 Laminates for a group exploring literatures of the American Southwest might include images of: uranium ore, rifles, the border with Mexico along the Rio Grande, Native Americans, the Roswell alien, 1950s television cowboys/girls, Anasazi ruins. Also quotations from writers whose work is associated with the region: Cormac McCarthy, Leslie Silko, Gloria Anzaldua, and Thomas Kenneally, for example.

2 In preparation for exploring the Nunnery Scene (3.1) in *Hamlet*, the group are given laminates of portrayals of Ophelia in art. These include paintings by John William Waterhouse (1894), John Everett Millais (1852) and Alexandre Cabanel (1883), as well as Victorian photographs of inmates of asylums dressed up to represent Ophelia. They are also given some key lines of text that are Ophelia's words or what is said about her. The task for the group is to present a theory about who Ophelia is and why she has such an iconic status in Western culture, despite her relatively small part in the play. The group then go on to create a 'circle of love' made of all the 'remembrances' Hamlet has given her and that her father has ordered her to return.

Elaboration

It is possible to add a further two stages to the process in which, first, participants form a tableau or **still-image** of their theory, and then, second, add movement through an improvised performance. It is possible, also, to conclude a **theory-building** exercise with a writing session in which participants articulate their theory in their smaller groups.

Unfinished materials

Description	An object, article of clothing, newspaper cutting, letter or opening to a story is introduced as a starting point for the development of a drama. The participants build on the clues and partial information offered in order to construct a drama to explore and develop themes, events and meanings suggested by the **unfinished materials**.
Cultural connections	Trailers for film and TV; geocaching; using augmented reality; adventure stories; lyrics; speculations on events behind the news; maps; diaries; using primary evidence in history; documentaries.
Learning opportunities	Encourages speculation, construction of narrative, collection of evidence; gives participants ownership over the development of the material by providing choices and the opportunity for the group's hypotheses to be worked through dramatically; requires detailed and extensive interpersonal negotiation and a collective approach to meaning-making.

Examples

1   As an introduction to work focusing on the experiences of children moved from children's homes in the UK to Australia in the 1940s and 1950s, participants are shown an authentic advertisement placed by an English social worker in an Australian newspaper. The advertisement asks for adults who were sent as orphaned children to Australia to contact the social worker with information about their experiences. The group use the advertisement as a starting point for imagining the roles of people who might respond to it and for devising scenes representing some of the experiences they might want to share with the social worker.

2   A class of 10/11-year-olds are introduced to *Romeo and Juliet* by a group of older students who show a series of tableaux from the play. The class are given the lines that the tableaux illustrate and are asked which figures they belong to. They then create scenes to link the tableaux together before looking at the whole play.

B. Narrative action

A day in the life

Critical events

Everywoman

Good angel/bad angel

Gossip circle

Hot-seating

Interviews/interrogations

Mantle of the expert

Meetings

Noises off

Overheard conversations

Reportage

Spotlighting

Tag-role

Teacher-in-role

Telephone/radio conversations

Time line

Time will tell

Will they – won't they?

Uses

These conventions are used to focus on significant events, incidents or encounters that will be central to the development of the narrative, or to introduce and develop plot. They allow groups to test out their hypotheses and speculations about the narrative through dramatic involvement; they involve individuals and groups moving the story on through the use of language and behaviour appropriate to the context.

Cultural origins

These are drawn from social conventions found in life, where behaviour is regularised and roles are observed, e.g. in meetings, courtrooms, interviews, family rituals. These are characterised by a natural use of time, space, presence and the experience of the conventions being lifelike (the term 'living-through' is sometimes associated with these conventions).

Level of demand

The nature of the conventions is generally recognisable to participants from their own life experience; the roles of actor and spectator tend to be clear even if they are interchangeable within the convention. Conventions may rely upon there being one or more individual who is prepared to risk themselves in role. This may depend on them feeling secure that spectators will value their role behaviour. The willingness to enter into action will be influenced by the level of interest and curiosity in the context or story as it unfolds. The naturalness of the conventions makes them a comfortable way of creating theatre for particular groups.

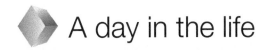 # A day in the life

Description	This convention works backwards from an important event in order to fill in the historical gaps in the story and to chart how the characters have arrived at the event. A chronological sequence is built up from scenes prepared by groups, involving the central character at various different times in the preceding 24 hours. After the scenes are run together, each scene in the sequence is subsequently redrafted to take into account the influence of other groups' scenes.
Cultural connections	A familiar form in novels, films and television; 'Draw my Life' YouTube phenomenon; build-your-own-story mobile games such as 'The Walking Dead'.
Learning opportunities	Drawing attention to the influences and exposing the forces that drive a character to a moment of conflict or decision; emphasising how inner conflicts and tensions shape the events and circumstances of the narrative.

Examples

1   A series of drama sessions had provided the opportunity for a group to discuss, as a community, issues relating to bullying and our social responsibility for those who bully and those who are their victims.

The work was based on some assumptions about effective learning in this important and sensitive area.

1   There are no easy answers or 'quick-fix' solutions to the problem and to pretend so is to cheat the participants who know the world to be an often difficult and complex place.
2   Rather, the drama should serve as a catalyst for public dialogue about the issue and its complexities.
3   Bullies are not born as bullies; they learn to be so. Therefore, they are also in a sense 'victims' whose lives need to be understood.
4   Drama will not change the hard bully any more than it will change the hard racist or bigot. But drama may well positively influence those on the edges – those who stand and watch and who are beginning to feel that maybe they should do something.
5   A drama about bullying should offer to mirror the complexities and contradictions of character, context and motive to be found both in life and the best literature.

The source of the drama was an actual letter written by a 14-year-old girl called Janet to a tabloid newspaper. In this letter she described how a gang of girls, led by Clare, was picking on her. The background to the situation was that Clare's mother worked in the same factory as Janet's mother. Janet's mother was a production line supervisor and she caught Clare's mother stealing, which led to her dismissal. This incident occurred recently and part of Clare's rage is to do with her mother being out of work and there being no money for Clare's birthday. Consequently, Janet has become the object of Clare's frustration and anger.

What appealed about this source was its complexity – it was not a simple and straightforward representation of bully and victim. It provided the opportunity to build sympathy, and therefore complexity, into the bully's situation as well as the victim's. The situation also encouraged consideration of how events that take place out of school may influence events in school.

Using **A day in the life**, the group created separate day-in-the-life sequences for both Clare and Janet, focusing on times during the day when they were either at home, at school or travelling. From these understandings of the characters, they then moved on to create scenes in which Janet and Clare met.

2   The group had started work with the following extract from Melvin Burgess' novel *Junk* (Andersen Press, 1996), written in the voice of the book's central character, Gemma:

> My parents are incompetent. They haven't got a clue. They think being a parent is like being an engineer or something – you do this, you do that, and this is the result you get at the other end.

> Someone ought to give parents lessons before they allow them to breed.

Using this convention, the group created separate day-in-the-life sequences for both Gemma and her parents, focusing on those times during the day when each of the characters was independent of the family. From these understandings of the characters, they then moved on to create scenes in which family interactions took place.

3   A group work on the themes in the Kathryn Bigelow's film *The Hurt Locker* by exploring Brian Turner's collection of poems *Here, Bullet* (Bloodaxe, 2007), one of the sources for the film that describes the Iraq war from a US soldier's perspective. They use these poems to create day-in-the-life sequences for a US Marine, an Iraqi child and a journalist in Iraq.

 # Critical events

Description	On the basis of their developing understandings of a character, group members identify **critical events** in the life of that character that lead the character to *either* a moment of 'effective surprise', generating the shock of new understanding (the moments chosen must clearly identify a point of discovery and the knowledge mastered) *or* a life's 'turning point', representing a clear moment of choice and decision-making. Whether decisions made are right or wrong, whether the consequences will be more or less than bargained for, whether the character understands the reasons for the choice made or not, are all immaterial at the point when the convention is used. However, these matters all await interrogation as the drama unfolds.
Cultural connections	Experimentation; problem-solving; discovery learning; spur-of-the-moment choices; non-linear games that use 'multiple choice dialogue' to allow the player to choose how the game develops; quick time events (QTEs).
Learning opportunities	Identifying moments of new understanding or the turning points in a character's life requires reflection and analysis of role and situation; offers insight into the character's present situation through the creation of their possible past and future; accentuates the relationships between cause and effect.

Example

1 And the rain that fell between us made — and still makes — a beaded curtain through which I saw, and will always see, my mother fading into the distance — borne away as on a ship. She didn't even wave goodbye. She simply stared at me and left me — abandoned.

> I looked at her and told myself I was an orphan, now. I decided, then and there, that — no matter how long my mother lived — she would never be my mother again. She was now her husband's widow, and though I do not think I could have known this then, I knew something like it; that I would never allow myself to be defined as someone's widow or as someone's mother but only — forever — as my *self*.

This example of 'effective surprise' from Timothy Findley's novel *The Telling of Lies* (Vintage, 1992) was taken as the starting point for an exploratory drama building from the extract's basic clues towards the creation of a fully realised **collective character**. The character was constructed by focusing on events created from the group's identification of further moments of effective surprise and likely turning points in the character's past, present and future.

 # Everywoman

Description	This convention gives the opportunity to bring together actors who are playing the same character at different points in that character's life. Collapsing space and time into a single and particular shared moment in time and space means that these multiple identities of the same character are free to exchange dialogue, advise, reminisce and interact, providing exemplary opportunities for insight and reflection.
Cultural connections	Narrative device in literature; voice-over in film, TV and radio broadcast reminiscing; older actor with younger self.
Learning opportunities	Requires extrapolation from existing understandings of character and motivation; offers opportunities for further insight into a character's likely life journey; provides a more detailed and rounded character for further exploration.

Examples

1   In a devised production based on Lewis Carroll's *Alice's Adventures in Wonderland* (Cambridge University Press, reprint edition, 2013) five actors of varying sizes, ages and heights, and wearing identical costumes, were used to play Alice. What began as a pragmatic solution to a technical problem (how to show Alice's shrinking and growing and to allow quick entrances) became a feature of the production. This lead to a number of occasions within the piece where all five Alices were present at the same time, enhancing the dream-like, other-world quality of the production, with four Alices offering advice from their own experience and dialoguing with the Alice who was faced with the dilemma.

2   Edward Albee's *Three Tall Women* (Josef Weinberger Plays, 2002) offers an accessible and readily available example of this particular convention in action. Albee calls his protagonist simply A: she is woman in her nineties. Albee describes her as 'thin, autocratic, proud, as together as the ravages of time will allow'. Two further female characters, B and C, are also present. C is there on behalf of A's law firm: she shows little compassion for A and has to be reminded by B (who is A's carer) that A represents C's future. At the end of Act 1 A has a stroke and Act 2 opens with what we assume is A – in fact a mannequin – lying in a bed. A then enters and the audience soon realise that B is a 52-year-old version of A, while C is a 26-year-old version of B. These three versions of the same woman are then able to dialogue and we come to understand that much of A and B's apparent melancholy with life is the result of a rift between the son and his mother(s) that has never been repaired.

Good angel/bad angel

Description	This convention is usually played out in multiples of three, where a central character faced with a moral dilemma is flanked by two angels who advise the character on a variety of courses of action from their respective standpoints of good and evil. At the culmination of the convention the character makes their decision.
	Generally there is no dialogue between the character and the angels, though it can make for interesting theatre if the angels are able to respond to one another.
Cultural connections	Notions of good and evil; right and wrong; the deceptions of tricksters; the advice of the great and the good.
Learning opportunities	Character becomes more aware of the problem and alternative courses of action; others become involved in and attempt to influence imminent action; slows the pace of the drama, providing a space for reflection.

Examples

1   The group were working on the creation of a village that was threatened by plague. At a village meeting they were informed that the first case of plague had been discovered in the village itself, and in role as the villagers they discussed what they should do. Some members of the village decided that they would not remain in the village any longer, despite the fact that this risked spreading the disease further in the surrounding countryside. **Good angel/bad angel** was set up for each of the villagers who wished to leave, and following this they were then free to make their personal decision.

2   I was really trying; believe me. But I just couldn't get it right. So every time I went in the door, I had to make a bigger and bigger effort to be the daughter they wanted me to be.

Starting from the piece of minimal text above, the group created a teenager, whom they called Ariyan. Exploring the reasons for the gulf between the young woman and her parents, the group had improvised a scene set at school between Ariyan and a teacher that resulted in Ariyan being presented with her annual school report. Certain that this was terrible, the scene ended with Ariyan sitting on a park bench with her report in her hand. What should she do? Open it? Destroy it? Hide it? Deliver it? Try and change what it said?

Good angel/bad angel was set up and following this, Ariyan made her decision.

 # Gossip circle

Description	This convention is a dramatised version of the game Whispers. Participants sit in a circle and the private and public behaviour of characters is commented upon by voicing aloud the rumours and gossip group members think might be circulating in a community. The object of the exercise is to deliberately exaggerate the rumour, expanding upon it as it is passed from person to person across the circle. The verbal exaggerations should be based within the realms of possibility and build on what is known of the character's likely behaviour – fantasising should be avoided. The final version of the rumour becomes the consensus view of other characters in the drama.
Cultural connections	Truth, lies and gossip; misunderstandings and deliberate slander and misrepresentation; online and tabloid 'celebrity' news and gossip columns.
Learning opportunities	Identifying tensions, conflicts and contradictions for further exploration; understanding the difference between the public and the private; devising and interpreting the behaviour of others.

Examples

1 A group have started working on Nigel Gray and Michael Foreman's *I'll Take You To Mrs Cole* (Macmillan, 1992) and the following extract has been read to them.

> When my mum came in from work and I hadn't got the table laid, she said, 'If you can't do what you're told, I'll take you to Mrs Cole.' Mrs Cole lives down the street, in a dirty house, in a noisy house, with lots of kids under her feet.

A **gossip circle** is set up to explore what people living in the neighbourhood might think about Mrs Cole.

2 The group are rehearsing for a story theatre performance of the old Danish myth of the changeling in which trolls substitute a troll baby for the baby of a farmer's wife. The woman decides to keep the baby, but as the child grows prejudices also begin to grow amongst members of the village. The group use **gossip circle** to build the comments and words of the villagers. They begin at a distance from the woman and her troll baby and as they draw nearer, their prejudices grow stronger and more direct. The group then **thought-track** the woman and child to discover what impact this has on them.

Hot-seating

Description	A group, working as themselves or in role, have the opportunity to question or interview role-player(s) who remain 'in character'. These characters may be 'released' from frozen improvisations or the role may be prepared and the role-player(s) formally seated facing questioners.
Cultural connections	Courts; inquiries; chat shows; media news; 'kiss and tell' articles; 'true life' confessions; online profiles; vines; celebrity Twitter accounts and celebrity profiles in media.
Learning opportunities	Highlighting character's motivations and personality disposition; encouraging insights into relationships between attitudes and events, and how events affect attitudes; encouraging reflective awareness of human behaviour.

Examples

1 A group have been speculating about what causes delinquency in some young adults. They have created a group of troublemakers who are causing havoc at their school. In order to discover more about the attitudes and motivations of the troublemakers, five volunteers take on their roles and are **hot-seated** by the rest of the group about attitudes to school, home, family, authority and so on.

2 A group have been reading a story about a family in which the stepson asks his stepfather to persuade his mother to allow him to keep pets. The mother determinedly takes no notice of the request; the group explore the likely conversation in pairs. Then the organiser in the role of stepfather places himself in the middle of the circle facing an empty chair with the stepson's jacket draped on it. He is **hot-seated** by the rest of the group role-playing the voice of the stepson, probing the stepfather's failure to get through to his mother.

Elaboration

In a drama exploring conservation issues, the group had focused on the problems of the deforestation of the South American rainforests. During a **hot-seat** session with the foreman of a logging company the group had become frustrated by the answers given. Did the character actually believe the answers he was giving or was he lying? Consequently, the questioners were given the option of physically **thought-tracking** the character if they felt a lie had been told, at which point they would be told the truth. This option does not necessarily guarantee a change in the answer on offer, since the truth is the truth. It does, however, help groups struggling to comprehend a value stance and mindset completely at variance with their own by removing any doubts about the veracity of what they hear.

Interviews/interrogations

Description	These are challenging, demanding situations designed to reveal information, attitudes, motives, aptitudes and capabilities. One party has the task of eliciting responses through appropriate questioning.
Cultural connections	Being in trouble; reporting to parents, employers, teachers, friends; detective stories; court cases; interviews for jobs; orals; news and documentary programmes; political broadcasts; flagging content online; Vlogs.
Learning opportunities	Framing appropriate questions and strategies; deciding on what information is required and on whether to trust the responses given; sequencing and piecing together of information; gives confidence and develops social skills necessary in real-life situations; contrasts outsider/insider views of events; a task-oriented activity.

Examples

1 In a study of Arthur Miller's play *The Crucible* (Methuen Drama, 2010) the group is split into pairs: in each pair, A is a television producer researching for a programme on witchcraft; B is a character from the play who may, or may not, wish to disclose information about their involvement in current events. After the interview A reports back to B in role, this time as his/her superior at the television station.

2 A group preparing for a drama concerned with exploring development strategies in underdeveloped nations are interviewed by UNICEF as to their skills, aptitudes, attitudes and past relevant experiences, so as to build up a picture of the value of voluntary aid. The group then interview other group members in the role of various flawed but enthusiastic volunteers, and have to decide on the abilities and give their assessment of each.

Mantle of the expert

Description	The group become characters endowed with specialist knowledge that is relevant to the situation: historians, social workers, mountain climbers. The situation is usually task-orientated so that expert understanding or skills are required to perform the task.
Cultural connections	Actual or media experience of teachers, social workers, historians, archivists, designers, builders, architects, carpenters, plumbers, doctors and so on; role-playing games; live action role-play; playing in the frame of video game characters.
Learning opportunities	Power and responsibility move from organiser to group; participants feel respected by having expert status; insights and understanding of different expert occupations are explored; provides distance from experience through professional codes/ethics.

Examples

1   The organiser is in the role of a senior executive for an international non-governmental organisation (NGO) concerned with climate change. The organiser (as senior executive) is concerned about a general lack of progress in informing the general public of the message of climate change and seeks the help of other senior staff within the organisation to produce a new, more effective campaign.

Take as a starting point the UN Secretary-General Ban Ki-moon's statement that 'There is no Plan B, because we do not have a Planet B' (a phrase that summarises the speech he delivered on 22 September 2014 at the Opening Day of Climate Week in New York City).

The group list all the skills, knowledge and understanding they possess in their expert roles and use these in order to design a campaign that really works. They then go on to produce the campaign

2   A group working on the theme of 'looking after older people' are invited, as 'experienced' architects, to research their needs. They then design and build a model of a suitable living environment for a group of seniors and present their findings to the organiser in role as a senior.

3   The group in role as 'landscape gardeners' are asked by the organiser as the Head Teacher of a Special School, to create a garden for her pupils, some of whom are visually impaired and some of whom use wheelchairs. The pupils are asked to use their

'expert' knowledge to design a suitable landscape for the garden and suggest appropriate planting so that all of the pupils can get enjoyment and access the garden. The Head Teacher also wants her pupils to be involved in looking after the garden.

In order for the landscape gardeners to present their plan to the Head Teacher, they must research: the needs of visually impaired and wheelchair-bound children; which flowers and plants might offer textures and smells for visually impaired people; how to design the garden so that it is interesting and accessible for wheelchair users; how sounds and textures might be used; how to design and build paths and beds so that wheelchair users can do some gardening themselves.

 # Meetings

Description	The group are gathered together within the drama to hear new information, plan action, make collective decisions and suggest strategies to solve problems that have arisen. The meeting may be chaired by the organiser or committee or other individuals – the group may meet without the organiser being present.
Cultural connections	Parliament; school meetings; assemblies; gang meetings; family discussions; parish council meetings; public inquiries; inquests; hustings; union meetings; picket lines; protest marches; Facebook groups; online forums, activist groups, gaming clans or guilds; conference calls; Google Hangouts.
Learning opportunities	Very structured, with the potential for a Chair to have control of proceedings; need to balance individual's needs and interests with other people's; emphasis on negotiation, bargaining, making a case; useful way of calmly considering alternatives and of starting/summarising a drama.

Examples

1   As a way of working on the theme of 'school', the group become the school staff and are told about the problems being caused within a particular class. The staff members are asked to recount problems that have occurred in their classrooms, and are then asked to suggest and evaluate strategies for dealing with the troublemakers.

2   Taking the following extract from Angy Feyisayo Jimba's novel *Stephanie's Little Flower* (Lulu Enterprises, 2012) as a starting point, the group have been looking at the plight of street children in Africa in general and on the streets of Lagos, Nigeria in particular.

> I don't have a mother whom I know
> I don't have a place which I can call my own
> Nobody cares for me whether I live or die
> A street child I am
>
> You say that I am dirty and not combed, not good to be seen.
> You say that I am mean and wild with a violent look.
> But I have had to fight to live
> I have to be strong to be alive.

As part of their exploration, the group, in role as aid workers, meet with and **hot-seat** an individual in role as one of the local street children, and then move on to organise a meeting of aid workers to discuss how best to help.

47

 Noises off

Description	The tension and motivation for the drama result from a sense of threat or danger that is imminent but not actually present. The group work with/against an imagined presence, e.g. they hide from an imagined enemy, or prepare for an important visitor. They are given orders/instructions from someone outside the drama whom they never meet face to face.
Cultural connections	Bogeymen; escape stories; following orders; 'outside pressure'; conventions in theatre and media drama.
Learning opportunities	Problem-solving and decision-making under pressure; cooperating to overcome a threat or perform a task; a good way of heightening tension and providing motivation.

Examples

1   A group is working on the story of Ishi – the last survivor of the Yahi, an American aboriginal tribe – who was kept as an exhibit in a museum for four and a half years from 1911. As curators, they know that Ishi is coming, but they have never met him. The task is to arrange the museum for his arrival and speculate on how he should be approached/looked after. The motivation for the work comes from a character who is not actually present but whose imminent arrival creates the tension for the drama.

2   A group are exploring a very brief scene from Caryl Churchill's play *Light Shining in Buckinghamshire* (Nick Hern Books, 1989). In this scene two young women, identified simply as 1st Woman and 2nd Woman, are discussing whether to leave a baby on the steps of a large manor house as both women are starving and the 1st Woman whose baby it is has no way to feed the child.

Actors playing the roles were finding it difficult to hit the right emotional tenor of the scene. **Noises off** was used as a rehearsal technique, which saw the group return to the scene and in groups of three **re-enact** it as written, but against the background of an armed guard on sentry duty. Very detailed and precise work resulted from the tension created by the introduction of this third character. The need to hold silences as the guard approached and to avoid histrionics in their dialogue had produced work of increased subtlety and had also demonstrated the possibilities inherent in a more restrained performance style.

Overheard conversations

Description	These conversations add tension or information to a situation that should not have been heard. The group might not know who the speakers are, or might only know one of the speakers. The conversation might be reported by spies, or be in the form of gossip and rumour. The group can go backwards or forwards in time to recreate key conversations that illuminate the present situation.
Cultural connections	Spies; rumour; gossip; celebrity magazines; eavesdropping – home, street, school, café; bugging; CB radio; Twitter scandal, MTV, BuzzFeed.
Learning opportunities	Devising/interpreting conversations that are relevant; speculating on the significance of what is heard; considering the truth of rumour; adding tension and secrecy as motivation within a situation.

Examples

1   A group are speculating on the causes of civil unrest in a state that has lost confidence in its leaders. Spies are sent out into different parts of the city to eavesdrop on the citizens. They return, and report what they have heard as a way of persuading the President to take the people's problems more seriously.

2   A group, as educational psychologists, are dealing with the problem of a young girl who is very clever but who has become totally withdrawn and aggressive. The organiser in the role of the young girl sits in the middle of a circle, while the group speak out overheard comments/conversations about her from friends, family, teachers and social workers.

 # Reportage

Description	This convention gives an interpretation/presentation of events through journalistic conventions and registers, in the manner of front-page stories, TV news or documentaries. The group may be in media roles or working outside the drama to represent what has happened from a distance, with an emphasis on how events can be distorted by outsiders.
Cultural connections	News stories; headlines; investigative journalism; tabloid press; Vlogs; YouTube personalities; 24-hour news channels; online newsfeeds, '10 most ...' lists online; Clickbait; radio bulletins; journalistic language; personal experience of the press at work.
Learning opportunities	Translation of events into news, selection of appropriate language and register; layout of headlines, story, picture; contrasting media genres – tabloid versus 'quality' press; TV versus radio.

Examples

1 A village is under threat from a proposed hydro-electric scheme. As a means of distancing them from their roles as villagers affected by the proposal, the group are reframed as journalists who are personally unaffected by the proposal, but who have the job of presenting both sides of the argument and reporting on the electricity company's publicity campaign and the villagers' protest activity.

2 A group working on the Vietnam conflict have been shown a copy of the famous Don McCullin photograph picturing a US marine suffering severe shell shock, who waits to be evacuated from the battle zone (taken in Hue, Vietnam, in February 1968). They present **still-images** of 'what that soldier might be seeing in his mind' – images of the jungle, of booby traps, helicopters, death, of families back home waiting for news.

Following these **still-images**, the group assume the roles of journalists who have returned from the war with these 'photographs'. The editor complains that they are 'unpatriotic' and bad for national morale. A discussion on the role of the press in wartime and the morality of armed intervention in the affairs of another country follows within the drama.

 # Spotlighting

Description	An imaginary spotlight is used to highlight particular activity within a whole group improvisation. The action in the wider group improvisation is frozen while the focus is placed upon an individual, pair or small group, who continue with their improvisation while the remainder of the group observe.
Cultural connections	Theatre and circus spotlights; searchlights; regional TV programmes that have a tight local focus; predictive computer search programmes that home in as one types.
Learning opportunities	Empathising with the motives and opinions of a character; exploring the differences between public and private utterances; analysing likely outcomes and the future direction of relationships and events.

Example

1 In many ways the ending of Shakespeare's *Measure for Measure* is unsatisfactory for a modern-day audience, leaving as it does a sense of unresolved issues.

In short, Vincentio, Duke of Vienna, believing that his city is ungovernable, pretends that he is leaving for Poland and names Angelo, whose 'blood is very snow-broth', as his deputy and replacement. In reality, the Duke remains in the city, disguised as Friar Lodowick, in order to observe Angelo's reign.

Angelo begins to enforce law and order strictly and in order to prove his determination, sentences a young man called Claudio to be executed. Claudio's sister Isabel intercedes for his life, but to no avail. The Duke watches and intervenes to save Claudio, but allows Isabel to believe that the death sentence has been carried out. All is revealed in the final act, and the Duke pardons everyone and assumes that everyone likewise pardons his own behaviour. Finally, despite having tricked Isabel in this way, the Duke assumes she will marry him, but Shakespeare does not give us her response to this 'semi-proposal' and the play ends without us hearing whether or not Isabel feels inclined to offer 'a willing ear'.

> ... Dear Isabel,
> I have a motion much imports your good,
> Whereto if you'll a willing ear incline,
> What's mine is yours, and what is yours is mine.
> So, bring us to our palace, where we'll show
> What's yet behind that's meet you all should know.

As a final activity a new, last scene entitled 'Dear Isabel, will you be my wife?' is created. For this activity, the group hypothesise about the content of these unscripted moments, and having searched for evidence in the actual text to support their hypothesis, create this final scene through improvisation, setting it during a celebration of the Duke's return. At different points during the improvisation characters are spotlit so that we can learn their personal thoughts, feelings and opinions both when in private conversation and also when interacting with Duke Vincentio.

Tag-role

Description	The participants in an improvisation can be 'tagged' (tapped on the palm of their hand by another group member) or appeal to be tagged (hand held out, palm upwards), and thereby be replaced in that improvisation by another group member. Any member of the audience group may decide to tag or respond to the performer's request to be tagged. The task is to keep the flow of the improvisation no matter how many people participate.
Cultural connections	Laser Tag; turn-based gaming; crowdsourcing; relay racing; physical education games; tagging on websites.
Learning opportunities	Enjoyable and fun activity; participants must accept rules; requires sensitivity and trust; collective responsibility for the construction of the narrative.

Examples

1 With a group new to drama who were nervous and unwilling to commit to extended improvisation, this convention was used to look at a simple scenario. Dad comes home with the surprise of two tickets to a football match, only to find Mum has two tickets to a concert on the same evening. Who goes where?

2 In a drama based on Mildred Taylor's *Roll of Thunder, Hear My Cry* (Puffin, new edition, 1994) the group recreates the moment when a black student named Little Man throws down the 'new' textbook he has been given in class, when he discovers a notice in the front of the book that shows that ten white students have used the book before it could be passed on to black students because of its poor condition.

   A group member as the teacher demands that Little Man pick it up. The group **tag-role** both Little Man and the teacher to see what the teacher might say to convince Little Man to pick up the book. They also consider Little Man's arguments and responses to what the teacher says.

3 In the Chinese legend of *Liang Zhu,* Liang persuades her father to let her disguise herself and go to school because it is forbidden for girls to go. The organiser in role as the father plays **tag-role** with volunteers from the group playing Liang. Initially the father forbids Liang to go, until group members, taking turns, build up a persuasive argument that changes his mind. The group then read Malala Yousafzai's 2013 speech to the United Nations about the importance of education for girls in the world, and think about the connections to Liang's situation and why some girls are prevented from getting equal educational opportunities to boys.

Teacher-in-role

Description	We use the generic term teacher-in-role (TiR) for this convention as this is the term by which the convention is best known. However, we appreciate that the convention may well be used by individuals who are not working in formal, educational contexts and who do not see themselves as teachers.
	The person taking responsibility as facilitator for the group manages the theatrical possibilities and learning opportunities provided by the dramatic context from *within* the context by adopting a suitable role in order to excite interest, control the action, invite involvement, provoke tension, challenge superficial thinking, create choices and ambiguity, develop the narrative and create possibilities for the group to interact in role. The organiser is not acting spontaneously but is trying to stimulate curiosity, enquiry and commitment to role and the issue being addressed through her involvement in the drama.
Cultural connections	Umpires/referees; team captains; coaches/trainers; moderators; online community managers; games masters; other adults who involve themselves in young people's play; artists-in-residence; other forms of open-ended interactive learning.
Learning opportunities	An opportunity for the group to work with the organiser on the inside of the drama, with experience being negotiated in role; chance for all participants to lay aside their actual roles and take on role relationships that have a variety of status and power variables.

Examples

1   The organiser initiates a drama about images of teenage disability in the following way. An empty chair is placed in a group circle; the group are asked to imagine that the chair is a wheelchair seen by its owner, John, as a possible block to him being as free as others. The organiser enters the circle in the role of Julie, a friend of John. She reads an imaginary letter (cf. **unfinished materials**) and asks the group to assess the relationship. The letter tells John that Julie is unhappy with the relationship, feels pressured and, as a result, won't go with him to a party on Saturday.

The organiser has composed and read the letter so that it creates the possibility of ambiguity about Julie's motives. Is it because she is embarrassed about her relationship when her friends are around? Is it because she is struggling to find the courage to deepen her relationship with John? Is it because John has spoilt a friendship by expecting more emotional commitment from Julie than she is prepared to give?

The group use **forum-theatre** to select and explore key moments that might reveal this ambiguity:

- Julie and John meeting Julie's friends while out shopping; exploration of Julie's and her friends' attitudes to John.
- Julie and John alone in John's house; exploration of what Julie means by being pressured.

The organiser maintains the role of Julie in order to sustain the ambiguity and develop it in response to the participants' handling of the situations. Various members of the group take the roles of John and others in each scene and are challenged/supported by the organiser (both in role as Julie and out of role as facilitator) as to the image of John they project.

The drama culminates in the party. The group decide on where John and Julie are placed, and then the party is improvised. The organiser uses the role of Julie as a way of encouraging the group to reconcile their understanding of the relationship through their roles as guests at the party by interacting with each other and with John and Julie.

2   As part of a drama that considers the social effects and consequences of the Alabama bus boycott of 1955, the group assume the roles of civil rights activists involved in a boycott march through Montgomery, Alabama. They encounter the organiser in role as an elderly black woman determined to catch the next bus. The group have to manage the encounter as if it were actually happening to them, which involves discovering and negotiating the limits of the action they are prepared to take in order to secure the success of their boycott.

Telephone/radio conversations

Description	These may be two-way conversations devised in pairs – to illuminate the present situation, or to break news, or to inform; or a one-way conversation, where the group only hear one side of the conversation. The organiser may use the convention to seek advice, create an outside pressure or introduce new information.
Cultural connections	Phone calls – bad news, surprises, conversations with friends or relatives, making excuses, calls for information; listening to others on the telephone; telephone conventions in thrillers/ detective stories; Txt abbreviations, e.g. LOL (laugh out loud); Skype; live stream software; in-game chat; Vlogs.
Learning opportunities	Devising appropriate dialogue; adding tension; deciphering/ interpreting information; matching register/ vocabulary to purpose of conversation; communicating without relying on gesture.

Examples

1   In a science fiction story a group of victims of persecution have found safe refuge on a new planet and have begun to rebuild their lives. They pick up a faint radio signal from an incoming spaceship. The spaceship comes from their persecutors' planet, which has been destroyed by war. The persecutors beg to be allowed to land and ask for forgiveness. What do the victims do?

2   A group of scientists and media people arrive in a remote community to investigate rumours that a UFO has landed nearby. They are escorted to the police station where the local sergeant feigns ignorance. She phones her superiors and, in the conversation that follows, there are clues that suggest that the sergeant knows more than she is saying. Eventually her superiors tell her to make the group sign the Official Secrets Act before anything more can be said.

Elaboration

This is a simple activity for work in pairs entitled **phone a friend**. The participants share/communicate news or developments in a story through a telephone conversation. Participants sit back to back so that the focus is on speaking and listening rather than on action or physical expression.

A **telephone tree** is set up between characters in a drama in order to discover if there are differing perspectives on key events. The sequence of calls can be pre-planned by the organiser, or the characters can determine the sequence.

 # Time line

Description	Having worked on a variety of small-group scenes both before and after a central dramatic encounter, volunteers are sculpted by the rest of the group to create an image representing the first few moments of this main scene. This image is then positioned centrally in the working space. The groups are then asked to stand a representative where they see their own small-group scene fitting in relation to its impact on, or time relationship with, the protagonists.
Cultural connections	Clocks; calendars; family trees; tables of historical events, presidents and prime ministers; the lineage of kings and queens; Facebook timeline and other social media history; 'previously watched' function on YouTube; 'suggested for you' advertising using one's internet history.
Learning opportunities	This convention allows us to physically represent how we see the relationship between more general events and a primary moment of concern, within either a piece of drama or a dramatic text.

Examples

1   In a drama exploring the breakdown of a marriage, subgroups had created a series of encounters, some of which showed courtship, blossoming and fading love, and eventual bitterness. Interestingly, in the **time line** moments that had appeared to be early courtship were placed after the actual breakdown of the relationship, thereby suggesting the possibility of a rapprochement.

2   Participants were given the following extract taken from Margaret Atwood's novel

The Handmaid's Tale (Virago, 1987):

> I admired my mother in some ways, although things between us were never easy. She expected too much from me, I felt. She expected me to vindicate her life for her, and the choices she'd made. I didn't want to live my life on her terms. I didn't want to be the model offspring, the incarnation of her ideas. We used to fight about that. I am not your justification for existence, I said to her once.

> I want her back. I want everything back, the way it was. But there is no point to it, this wanting.

Working from this stimulus they were asked to create a series of **still-images** as though they were photographs of important moments from the past, contained in a photo album lying forgotten in a desk drawer. Having created and shared these images with appropriate captions, they were then time-lined.

 # Time will tell

Description	This convention specifically addresses the question: What if? Through the construction, realisation and exploration of a predictive scene based on current circumstances, the group pose questions around future behaviour and explore the consequences of unchanging behaviour and attitude.
Cultural connections	*Doctor Who*; time tunnels; alternate universes; prophecy and fulfilment; time heals the heart.
Learning opportunities	Events are extrapolated from existing analysis of character and current patterns of behaviour; selection and realisation of significant future moments; provides a more complex character for additional exploration.

Examples

1   In a drama exploring the relationships within a dysfunctional family comprising mother, father, sister and younger brother, the group projected ahead to a point ten years in the future.

The group had decided that the family's relationships were driven by suspicion, envy and a lack of charity. The scene created was at the father's funeral. The whole group attended in role as distant relatives and everyone's eyes were on the three family members. When the funeral concluded without any contact between the three principals, the group decided that this was only one of many possible futures. Looking both backwards and forwards in time, they sought to construct a more positive future.

2   The group had been looking at a traditional story that told of two brothers who each farmed the land to either side of a narrow river. One of the brothers became increasingly jealous of his sibling and his actions became more and more petty, such that one day, when an itinerant carpenter came to his farm asking for work, he pointed the carpenter towards a pile of wood and told him to build a high fence along the riverbank so that he would no longer need to see his brother's farm.

On the day the carpenter left, the farmer discovered that the carpenter had built not a wall but a bridge!

Ten years in the future, had anyone crossed that bridge?

Will they – won't they?

Description	A large sheet of paper is divided into 4 columns. The first column entitled **Possible** is open for the immediate and general collection and listing of ideas concerning what initially seem the possible courses of action open to a particular character in a drama. All ideas are listed without discussion of their strengths and weaknesses.
	The next two columns are headed **Most Probable** and **Impossible**.
	Focusing around the **Possible** category, the group discusses their initial ideas and views on the varying courses of action they see available to a character. On the basis of how likely they eventually feel each particular response might be, they shift ideas from their list in the first column and enter them under either **Most Probable** or **Impossible**.
	Then, starting with the ideas listed in the **Most Probable** column, the group members test out the alternatives through improvisation, seeking the most satisfactory outcome. In the course of their improvisations they are free to deliberate on outcomes and to move ideas back and forth between the columns as their explorations provide satisfactory answers. Ideas tested in action and agreed by the group are then placed in the final column headed **Actual**.
Cultural connections	Testing the water; straw polls; collaboration rather than competition.
Learning opportunities	Critical thinking and problem-solving; communication and collaboration; choosing and expressing analysis of human action and interaction.

Example

1 The organiser as the Mother (**teacher-in-role**) performs the following monologue for the group.

> Listen. They say you should never have regrets. Regrets don't change anything. Just give you sleepless nights. But if I could have that moment over again, I would. I'd do it differently.
>
> People said we were too much alike. But parents are responsible, aren't we? If we're not, who is? We're here to love her; meant to help her. That's all I ever meant to do. Help her. But the more I tried, the less help I was.

But it wasn't always like that. We had our good times too. And for a long, long time we were best friends. Her Dad wasn't much of a traveller, but we made up for it and we always brought him a postcard home. Kept them! Always reckoned we'd beat the postman home, and anyway it gave more room to write.

Now, I'm just so tired of looking for answers, tired of the blame game ... blaming me ... blaming her Dad ...blaming Reesa. All I want is for it all to be over ... for us to have a chance of starting again.

Coming out of role and without offering the group the opportunity to **hot-seat** the organiser then sets up **taking sides** to see where the group stand in relation to the Mother and Reesa and as a means of focusing both discussion and reflection.

Following this convention, in which the group are fairly evenly split, the organiser hands out the postcards that were mentioned in the Mother's speech, one per group of 4 or 5 participants, and asks these sub-groups to create the happy times that they represent.

Having shared this work and **time-lined** the postcards, the organiser returns to the original monologue and reminds the group of the line: 'But if I could have that moment over again.'

The group are then asked to consider that moment. What **Possible** event might this moment have been? What did Reesa do? What did her Mother do?

Their various exploratory suggestions and then the group's decisions are charted as they reflect on possibilities and try out ideas in action. Finally, when the moment of crisis has been determined, **forum-theatre** is used to see if there is a way in which the future could be saved.

C. Poetic action

Action narration	Masks
Alter ego	Mimed activity
Analogy	Montage
Behind the scene	Physical theatre
Caption-making	Play within a play
Ceremony	Prepared roles
Chamber theatre	Readers' theatre
Come on down!	Re-enactment
Commedia dell'arte	Reminiscence theatre
Cross-cutting	Revue
Documentary theatre	Ritual
Flashback	Role-reversal
Folk-forms	Shape-shifting
Forum-theatre	Small-group play-making
Genre switch	Soundscape
Gestus	TV times
Living newspaper	Verbatim theatre

Uses

These conventions are useful as a means of looking beyond the storyline, or as a means of making a deliberate shift from the realism of narrative conventions to conventions that heighten awareness of form and that allow for the exploration and representation of key symbols and images suggested by the work. The effect of moving into poetic action is often to:

- bring a fresh perspective to work that is becoming stale or dominated by plot-level thinking
- open up an alternative channel of communication that works at the level of symbolic interpretation
- increase emotional involvement.

Cultural origins

These are drawn from performing arts conventions and either make an elastic, often stylised, use of time, space and presence to consciously communicate symbolic intent (e.g. **masks**, **ritual**) or are used out of their predictable context and allow for incongruities and discords (e.g. **come on down!**).

Level of demand

Some groups express a preference for working poetically – that is in an obviously theatrical way – rather than narratively, which can feel uncomfortably close to actual living. Poetic conventions often require a disciplined crafting of speech and action; the mode of communication is highly selective and bound by the constraints of the convention. Some of the conventions are complex to operate and require clear agreements about actor/spectator roles (e.g. **montage**).

Action narration

Description	A scene is performed with participants using **narration** to describe their actions around individual spoken lines of dialogue. As a further step, having first practised the initial approach, the participants can be asked to define each action of the narrative by adding a suitably descriptive adverb.
Cultural connections	Preplanning of play activities; rehearsal for difficult encounters in 'real life'; commentary over live streaming.
Learning opportunities	Using this technique slows action down, thereby encouraging intense and focused scrutiny of events. In particular, by slowing the pace of violent events the convention allows for a cooler and more distanced perspective.

Examples

1 A group of actors were working on a production of Harold Pinter's *The Caretaker* (Faber & Faber, 1991). Act 2 of the play contains the following:

> ASTON. Here you are. (ASTON *offers the bag to* DAVIES.)
> MICK *grabs it*. ASTON *takes it*.
> MICK *grabs it*. DAVIES *reaches for it*.
> ASTON *takes it*. MICK *reaches for it*.
> ASTON *gives it to* DAVIES. MICK *grabs it*.
> *Pause*.
> ASTON *takes it*. DAVIES *takes it*. MICK *takes it*. DAVIES *reaches for it*. ASTON *takes it*.
> *Pause*.
> ASTON *gives it to* MICK. MICK *gives it to* DAVIES.
> DAVIES *grasps it to him*.
> *Pause*.
> MICK *looks at* ASTON. DAVIES *moves away with the bag*.
> *He drops it*.
> *Pause*.
> *They watch him. He picks it up. Goes to his bed, and sits*.

In rehearsal the actors reached a block with this routine until **action narration** was added. For example:

> ASTON. I say 'Here you are' to Davies and offer him the bag.

Finally the scene was replayed with all the **action narration** sequences stripped out.

2 In a drama based on the story of a troubled marriage, the group create the scene in which one of the partners decides that the

marriage must end. The scene is played out twice with each partner giving their own contrasting **action narration** of the events – 'I came home, early, the whole house seemed to be filled with her friends … all they were doing was gossiping.' – 'Paul burst in, sulking as usual, he made a fuss about me having a few friends round.' The actors have to replay the scene twice to reflect the differences in the two **narrations**.

 # Alter-ego

Description	In this convention, essentially an extension of **thought-tracking**, participants work in pairs, one as the character and one as that character's thoughts. The double's function is to provide a commentary of 'inner speech', focusing thoughts and feelings against which the protagonist plays out their surface action and dialogue as though their **alter ego** was not there (cf. **shape-shifting**).
Cultural connections	Shadows; anonymous blogs; 'trolling'; 'flaming'; online personas; voice-over commentaries; 'stiff upper lip'; hiding one's true feelings; text and subtext in any form of drama.
Learning opportunities	This convention is designed to deepen the collective understanding of the ways a character might be feeling in a given situation, even though the character might not be able publicly to admit or express those feelings. Devising 'inner speech' requires critical analysis of situation and role; concretising subtext generates an affective response, accentuating the influence of context on human behaviour.

Examples

1   In the fictional world created by Ray Bradbury in his novel *Fahrenheit 451* (1953) the Fireman's job is to start fires in order to burn books. Ideas are as dangerous as questions. 'If you don't want a man unhappy politically, don't give him two sides to a question to worry him; give him one. Better yet, give him none', as Fire Chief Beatty explains to Montag. But Montag is beginning to doubt: 'in the old days, before homes were completely fireproofed … Didn't firemen prevent fires rather than stoke them up and get them going?' Participants improvise an apparently mundane conversation about work between Montag and Beatty in which the actors playing **alter egos** show that the superficial, surface dialogue masks both Beatty's growing suspicions about Montag's loyalty and Montag's fear of being found out.

2   As a way of exploring the gap between what is said and what is meant in an argument between a girl and her mother, two 'shadows' stand with the characters and speak aloud the girl's and the mother's thoughts during the dialogue.

3   In rehearsing the Nunnery Scene from William Shakespeare's *Hamlet* (3.1), Hamlet and Ophelia have 'shadows' who physically reflect the character's real feelings during the scene. As well as playing the scene naturalistically, the shadows then perform the scene silently on their own as **physical theatre**.

 # Analogy

Description	A problem is revealed through working on a parallel situation that mirrors the real problem – usually used where the real problem is too familiar, full of prejudice or likely to make participants feel threatened or exposed. The convention encourages objective analysis of the analogous situation and then for connections to be made between the unfamiliar and the actual.
Cultural connections	Myths; legends; fairy stories; metaphors; similes.
Learning opportunities	Creating and analysing metaphors; indirectly handling sensitive/controversial issues; making connections between **analogy** and real problems, encouraging reflection and providing distance for new learning about old material.

Examples

1   A participatory drama exploring real-world persecution on Earth is represented as a science fiction story concerning a group of space travellers fleeing from one planet to find another where they can be safe. A planet is selected as a new homeland, and word is sent to all who are persecuted on other planets to come to it. However, the new planet is already home to people who do not share the same beliefs as the newcomers.

2   A group prepare a participatory drama workshop for 6-year-olds, focusing on green issues. They create an **analogy** for pollution through a prophecy told in polar lands. The last of the great dragons is imprisoned beneath the ice. The prophecy goes on to warn that: 'When the ashes fall from the south, and the snow turns to stinging rain, then the dragons will fly again.' At the beginning of the workshop time is devoted to helping the children into role as villagers who live in the green lands on the edge of the ice and creating a village structure supported by members of the visiting group. Once these roles are established, the 6-year-olds are visited by an explorer who brings the news that the prophecy is being fulfilled.

Behind the scene

Description	A private or intimate scene is played against the background of larger social and historical events. Groups prepare both an intimate and a historical scene and, when ready, they form two circles for performance – an inner intimate circle with the historical circle surrounding. The scenes are then run simultaneously. However, the first time through we hear only the soundtrack from the intimate scene; then, played for a second time, we again see both scenes, but hear only the soundtrack from the historical scene.
Cultural connections	Historical films and romantic fiction; Brecht's plays; film conventions; the history of social media trending; 'Where were you when …' pages.
Learning opportunities	Understanding the relationship between private and public events; putting events into a social and historical perspective; exploring the influences of history on private lives.

Examples

1 Henry Longfellow's poem *Evangeline* tells the love story of Evangeline and Gabriel, set against the ethnic cleansing of the Acadiennes people of Nova Scotia by the British in 1755. On the day that they announce their engagement the British burn their village and force the people onto ships to be deported. The couple are separated and Evangeline spends the rest of her life trying to find Gabriel. They finally meet again at his deathbed.

Groups prepare two connected scenes. The couple's courtship is set against the growing friction and trouble between the Acadiennes and the British soldiers. The **montage** of scenes makes the participants consider whether the couple were 'blind' to what was happening and puts the original romantic poem back in its historical context.

2 Participants working on William Shakespeare's *Romeo and Juliet* consider the nature of the feud between the Capulets and Montagues. They improvise scenes showing incidents from the feud and the effect of the feud on everyday life in Verona. These scenes are then played behind intimate scenes from the play. Thus, as Juliet speaks with the nurse, her father plots in the background to rob a Montague ship; the balcony scene is played against a gang discussion about finding and attacking Romeo; the opening market 'bite my thumb' scene is played with unnamed characters representing children, market traders and others trying to go about their business in the market.

Caption-making

Description	Groups devise slogans, titles, chapter headings and verbal encapsulations of what is being presented visually. They are asked to crystallise their work within a phrase; or to work to a given title; or to summarise a scene in words; or to fit a caption to another group's work. Classifying these captions in terms of anchors, relays and riddles can further refine the use of captions. An 'anchor caption' is one intended to help the spectator 'read' a dramatic moment by supplying a direct and literal definition of its meaning. A 'relay caption' complements the drama by creating a reciprocal relationship between caption and event where each sheds light on the other. A 'riddle caption' offers a mysterious or enigmatic comment that provokes the spectator into questioning their initial response. (For further details see Clark, J. *et al.*, *Lessons for the Living*, Mayfair Cornerstone, 1997.)
Cultural connections	Advertisements; posters; jingles; Buzzfeed; Clickbait; YouTube video titles; generating a hit rate; naming a channel; episode titles on TV series; portrait and sculpture titles; song titles; album titles; chapter headings.
Learning opportunities	Precision of description; selection of appropriate form and language; making a reflective analysis of experience in order to identify its essence; summarising experience.

Examples

1 **Anchor caption** In an investigative drama looking at recruitment into the armed services, a group devise First World War recruitment posters, after considering authentic examples. As the groups show their posters, the observers have to suggest captions for the image presented. The same exercise is repeated in relation to present-day advertisements, so that a comparison between recruitment in wartime as opposed to peacetime can be considered.

2 **Relay caption** In a drama concerned with the strains within a family, the group created a sequence of images to represent family photographs taken at the son's wedding. One such image showed the son dancing closely with one of the bridesmaids, watched closely by other family members. The relay caption read: 'Forsaking all others'.

3 **Riddle caption**

> So the baby was carried in a small deal box, under an ancient woman's shawl, to the churchyard that night, and buried by

lantern-light, at the cost of a shilling and a pint of beer to the sexton, in that shabby corner of God's allotment where He lets the nettles grow ...

The group had worked from the brief extract above, taken from Thomas Hardy's *Tess of the D'Urbervilles*, to create the character of the old woman whose shawl had been used to cover the baby's coffin. Tracking the woman back through her earlier life experiences, they constructed a series of **still-images** that culminated in the image of the sexton handing the shawl back to the old woman following the baby's burial. In this final image, the old woman stood lost in memory, her gaze held by the shawl. The group captioned the image: 'Ghosts from the Past'.

Ceremony

Description	Groups devise special events to mark, commemorate or celebrate something of cultural/historical significance.
Cultural connections	Weddings; civil partnerships; naming ceremonies; cross-cultural ceremonies; graduations; religious ceremonies; funerals; remembrance and feast days; birthdays.
Learning opportunities	Devising appropriate activity to mark something that has occurred or is about to occur in the drama; may involve performance work; reflective attitude combined with celebratory experience; easily controlled, structured activity; involvement of whole group; useful as a conclusion or review.

Examples

1 In a drama looking at 'the effects of change', a group 'build' a village. In order to give the group a sense of the village's history, they are asked to devise a **ceremony** to celebrate the unveiling of a newly commissioned war memorial. The work includes making images to represent the memorial, writing captions for it, devising speeches, choosing the music/songs to be played and devising contrasting contributions from young people, veterans and newcomers to the village.

2 A parcel of patterns brought the plague to Eyam. A parcel sent up from London to George Vicars, a journeyman tailor, who was lodging with Mrs. Cooper in a cottage by the west end of the churchyard.

So begins Jill Paton Walsh's *A Parcel of Patterns* (Puffin, 1994), her fictional account of how the village of Eyam in England's Derbyshire Dales struggled against an outbreak of the Great Plague in 1665. The group explored the situation as described in the novel by creating a fictional Eyam and taking on the roles of its villagers. By way of closing the drama, the group created a **ceremony** tinged with sadness for the loss of friends but also celebrating their own survival.

3 A group are deepening their understanding of the story of Sleeping Beauty. They begin by recreating the naming feast and decide on what fairy roles they will take – the fairy of dreams, of health, of good fortune and so on. They each make a gift for the newborn child to protect her. They also prepare the feast by making place settings and table decorations, thinking about who will sit where. A group member in the role of the King enters, welcomes the fairies and they begin the **ceremony** of placing their gifts in the baby's crib and making a wish. The organiser breaks up the **ceremony** in the role of the Fairy of the North **teacher-in-role**), who was not invited to the **ceremony** and who now promises revenge.

Chamber theatre

Description	This convention, a variation of **readers' theatre**, allows the dramatic presentation of material not originally written for performance. Novels and stories are the best source of material for **chamber theatre** and any suitable source will inevitably contain a good deal of **narration**. **Chamber theatre** requires a narrator, who as the central character, delivers his or her own thoughts, feelings and actions while other group members act out what the narrator is describing, either through mime, a mixture of mime and dialogue, or by speaking aloud the **narration** and dialogue that applies to each of their own characters.
Cultural connections	A central approach in children's game-playing; the sharing of jokes and stories.
Learning opportunities	Devising enacted sequences and the chosen balance between dialogue and **narration** requires reflection, selectivity and a strong sense of the dramatic; developing confidence in group work and expressive performance in an activity controlled by the content and form of the **narration**.

Example

1   A group working on a **chamber theatre** performance piece based on the power of story begin their devising process by looking at the following extract from Terry Pratchett's *Witches Abroad* (Corgi, 2005).

> People think stories are shaped by people. In fact, it's the other way round.

> Stories can exist independently of their players. If you know that, the knowledge is power.

> Stories ... have been blowing and uncoiling around the universe since the beginning of time. And they have evolved. The weakest have died and the strongest have survived and they have grown fat on the retelling ...

> And their very existence overlays a faint but insistent pattern on the chaos that is history. Stories etch grooves deep enough for people to follow in the same way that water follows certain paths down a mountainside. And every time fresh actors tread the path of the story, the groove runs deeper ...

> So a thousand heroes have stolen fire from the gods. A thousand wolves have eaten grandmother, a thousand princesses have been kissed ...

Stories don't care who takes part in them. All that matters is that the story gets told, that the story repeats.

Using this extract as an opening **narration**, the group created a theatre piece that explored the notion of universal truths and cultural symbiosis. Taking stories from around the world, the group performed narrative extracts emphasising cultural similarities and switching between stories and cultures with playful intent. For example, they explored the notion of greed and its consequences through selected excerpting from Charles Dickens' *A Christmas Carol*, Liana Romulo's 'A Feast of Gold' from *Filipino Children's Favorite Stories* (Tuttle Publishing, 2000) and the Somaiah's 'Munna and the Grain of Rice' from *Indian Children's Favourite Stories* (Tuttle Publishing, 2006).

Come on down!

Description	As a way of bringing fresh insights to a passage of action that has become stale or sentimental, a radical shift of style is introduced so that the action is translated into a popular form such as a game-show format, circus routine, chat show, soap opera, pop video, computer game, mobile app, interactive exhibit and so on.
Cultural connections	Immediate experience of examples such as those given above.
Learning opportunities	Reveals implicit style of original action through contrast with popular style introduced; forces re-examination of values in original action as well as those embedded in popular form itself; needs a selective translation of the original action into the constraints of new form.

Examples

1 In *Trafford Tanzi* (*Plays One*, Oberon Modern Playwrights, 1996) Claire Luckham translates issues relating to gender and gender expectations into the form of a wrestling match.

2 A group working on the theme of 'Education' represent the pressures of the examination system through the form of a horse race, complete with appropriate hurdles, obstacles and commentary.

3 As part of an issue-based drama looking at housing problems, events are acted out in the manner of a Chinese Monkey legend, a West African Anansi story and/or as part of the Indian epic Ramayana.

Commedia dell'arte

Description	With its probable roots in the comedic theatre of Ancient Rome, this improvised comic theatre form originating in 16th-century Italy provides us today with an invaluable resource of scripts, scenarios, *Lazzi/Meccanismi* ('gags' or stock jokes and comic routines) and stock characters whose roles, characteristics and costumes are well defined. Today, almost eight hundred scenarios have survived in outline form and are available on the Web and in translation. These materials provide an ideal basis for a variety of improvisation, devising and rehearsal approaches.
Cultural connections	Silent movies: Chaplin, Keaton, and Lloyd; cartoons – in particular *The Simpsons* and Warner Bros; clowns and clowning; Punch and Judy; stock characters such as Joey in *Friends* and Kramer in *Seinfeld*.
Learning opportunities	Fun; physical discipline, spontaneous and innovative use of the imagination; collaboration and cooperation.

Example

1   Actors were working on the early stages of a production of Molière's *Les Fourberies de Scapin* (literally, Scapin's Deceits), a joyous farce, the plot of which involves two young men, Octave (son of Argante) and Leandre (son of Geronte), who, while their fathers are away on business, fall in love with two women, Hyacinte and Zerbinette. Problems arise when Argante and Geronte, the two domineering, miserly fathers, return and announce that they have marital plans for their respective sons. Fortunately, Scapin, Leandre's clever servant, is happy to step in and foil the fathers' plans and ensure the happiness of the young people. Scapin sets in motion a devious plot to persuade the fathers that they really don't want what they do want and, in fact, do want what they don't want. In the end it turns out that Hyacinte is actually Geronte's daughter and the wife that Argante had in mind for Octave all along; and Zerbinette is actually Argante's long-lost offspring whom he had always intended to be Leandre's bride. So true love does triumph after all and even Scapin, who has tricked them all several times over, is forgiven.

Molière drew the character of Scapin from **Commedia dell'arte** and much of the play's humour comes from an exploration of master/servant relationships. Therefore, before casting and before an introduction to the text proper, the actors explored **Commedia dell'arte** characters, in particular:

- Vecchi – Master characters, nobles.
- Pantalone – The master, who in many storylines attempts to control his household and protect his money from cunning servants.
- Innamorati – These characters are usually the daughters and sons of the Vecchi, and thus enjoy high status. They almost always create the play's dilemma.
- Zanni – Servant character.
- Arlecchino (Harlequin) – The most popular and famous character to come out of **Commedia dell'arte**.
- Pantalone's witty servant and prankster.

Improvisations around these characters were often undertaken using Grommelot – the 'babble-speak' of **Commedia dell'arte**, which uses intonation, rhythm and accent coupled with emotion and bodily action to create a babble of sounds that, nevertheless, manage to convey the sense of the meaning of a speech. *Lazzi* were often used as the basis of improvisation, and specific *lazzi* with an emphasis on rebellion and social class were explored, such as:

- **The Statue:** In this *lazzo* Arlecchino is brought on stage as a statue. He plays tricks on the other characters while their backs are turned, but always returns to his original position when they turn to face him.
- **Madness:** A lovelorn character pretends to be insane so they can scare others by their behaviour and ranting in an attempt to avoid an arranged marriage or to gain access to their true beloved.
- ***Lazzo* of searching:** Two young people are trying to find each other. As soon as one leaves the stage, the other appears. This is repeated several times at once or throughout the play, often with shouting for each other, and direct complaints to the audience.
- ***Lazzo* of the *Battocchio*:** This *lazzo* features the *battocchio*, or slapstick. The slapstick is made from two pieces of wood fitted together so that they create a slapping sound and is used in comic 'beatings'.
- ***Lazzo* of Counting Money:** The Zanni divides Pantalone's money between Pantalone and himself in the following way: one for Pantalone, two for me (gives a single coin to Pantalone and two to himself); two for Pantalone, three for me, and so on.

The intention in all of this work was to free up the actors, creating a spontaneous and imaginative response to character, situation and context before casting and exploring Molière's text proper, and this lead to a more nuanced performance.

This approach could be used with texts as diverse as Aphra Behn's plays *The Rover* and *The Emperor of the Moon*, Bertolt Brecht's *The Resistible Rise of Arturo Ui*, Nicolai Erdman's *The Suicide*, Carlo Goldoni's *A Servant of Two Masters* and much of the work of Dario Fo, and so on.

Cross-cutting

Description	Participants devise and rehearse two or more scenes, which occur at different times and in separate places. They then work on cutting backwards and forwards between the two scenes, editing them so as to carefully maximise the links, comparisons, analogies and similarities or ironic contradictions that exist between the two (cf. **montage**).
Cultural connections	A familiar device in film and television, split-screen gaming; Skype and other conference-calling software; Screen Sharing; mirroring software.
Learning opportunities	Consideration of, and experimentation with, the relationship between form and content; heightened collective expression; the potential for the discovery of new meanings through the intercutting, combining and juxtaposition of action/dialogue, and so on.

Examples

1 Earlier in the drama, participants had been in role as the people living in a small village in the harsh remoteness of the Scilly Isles, some 200 years ago. The unforgiving climate and hard life meant that some people in those days sought to better their lifestyle by wrecking ships for the profits to be had from salvage. Such wreckers placed false beacons on the cliff tops to lure unsuspecting ships to their doom on the rocks. All those in the village, whether active wreckers or not, are in some way implicated in this way of life. Now, participants work in groups to prepare and **cross-cut** two scenes, one of which shows the hasty, night-time preparations for a wrecking, while the other shows the slow, methodical routine of unsuspecting passengers and crew on board the fated ship.

2 Reflecting on a series of sessions looking at the plight of child labour in developing countries, participants summarise their understandings in a short performance piece that includes a sequence **cross-cutting** between a simple children's game and a scene encapsulating the repetitive drudge of a factory assembly line.

Documentary theatre

Description	The selection of historical or factual material from either past or current events. **Documentary theatre** involves the analysis of two essential types of information: either primary source (eyewitness accounts of relevant events) or secondary source (interpretations or retellings of events by people not present at the time). Following analysis and research and the exploration of possibilities through other selected drama conventions, sources are translated into dramatic form while staying as truthful as possible to these original materials.
Cultural connections	Docudrama on film and television; Twitter Breaking News; mobile phone eyewitness accounts; use of Facebook to organise political protest, and so on.
Learning opportunities	Researching significant material; selecting material for its dramatic potential; extrapolating and interpreting likely colour and detail from sources without distorting factual content; translating material into dramatic form; sequencing.

Examples

1   During their work on the Suffragette Movement a drama group researched suffragettes who put their own freedom and lives at risk through militant action, subsequent hunger strikes and force-feeding. (Suffragettes were members of the women's movements in the late 19th and early 20th centuries who fought for the right to vote.) They became particularly interested in the case of Emily Wilding Davison, who died in front of the king's horse at the Derby in 1913, and created a series of scenes exploring the vexed question of whether she actually intended to sacrifice herself or simply make a protest.

2   A group devises a docudrama for live performance based on the stories and other writings of migrants of today and from history. They research their own families and communities to generate the material for performance and script the piece using as much original material (oral history) as possible. The docudrama reflects the personal family experiences of the group as well as the broader experience of those migrants who have been the engine of their city's history. The docudrama also reflects the different performance traditions associated with the diverse cultures represented in the stories told. In addition to the performance the group also organise a major foyer display of photos, memories, maps and other artefacts related to the theme.

 # Flashback

Description	Scenes are created that predate an important moment in the drama, so that images from the past help to explicate or reinforce the relationship between the dramatic present moment and its history. **Flashback** scenes can be inserted into the unfolding of a scene in present time or, at a crucial moment, can be used to confront a central character with recollections of their past.
Cultural connections	Common storytelling device in all other narrative genres.
Learning opportunities	Extrapolation from reflective analysis of character and current patterns of behaviour; selection and realisation of significant moments of prior experience; provides a more detailed and complex character for further exploration.

Examples

1   A character had been presented to the group whose most significant possession was an old and battered suitcase. The suitcase appeared to be filled with a collection of somewhat unlikely objects: toy car, Christmas bauble, camera, box of badges, string, cassette tape, snow shaker, photograph of a child, whistle, penknife, torn postcard. In a series of **flashbacks** the group were asked to show those past moments when the character first chose and collected each of these objects and who was with them at the time. The sequence of events was then **time-lined** into chronological order by deciding on the age of the character in each group's scene.

2   As part of a project exploring mother-and-daughter relationships the group had discovered the following extract from Anne Enright's novel *The Wig My Father Wore* (Jonathan Cape, 1995):

> Upstairs my mother finds me looking at a new picture on the wall. It is a picture of her, with a baby in her arms. The baby is me. She sits in the grass and holds me up for the camera, mother-love in her face and love for the person taking the picture in her eyes.
>
> 'Why did you put that up?' I say to her.
>
> 'Grow up, Grainne,' she says, on her way to the bathroom.
>
> 'I'm in that picture.'
>
> 'I would have thought', she says, 'that was the point.' 'Who took it?' I say. 'Did Da take that?'

'Who do you think?' she says as she closes the door.

She stays in the bathroom too long, while my father sings downstairs and Phil sits in silence. My mother cries privately but with no shame. She cries easily, because it is her right to cry, in her own bathroom, in her own life. She cries quietly, and with abandon, because her tears, like her children, are her own.

Having enacted the above encounter, the group created a series of **flashback** moments as images in the mind of Grainne as she stood listening and remembering, standing before the new picture.

3   As preparation for rehearsing the Nunnery Scene in William Shakespeare's *Hamlet* (Act 3, Scene 1), the actors work in pairs to make a 'circle of love' around Ophelia made up of all the 'remembrances' she must now return to Hamlet.

> OPHELIA
> My lord, I have remembrances of yours
> That I have longèd long to re-deliver.
> I pray you now receive them.

The pairs create these 'remembrances', which include objects, poems and keepsakes made from art materials and then create through mime the **flashback** moment when their chosen remembrance was first exchanged between Hamlet and Ophelia. The **flashbacks** are then placed in a 'circle of love' around the organiser in role as Ophelia (**teacher-in-role**), who reflects on their importance to her and how painful it will be to return them.

Then the group consider how Ophelia might now read the love letter from Hamlet – 'Doubt thou the stars are fire'. How might the events since Hamlet went to Wittenberg have changed his love for her?

Folk-forms

Description	The group may devise traditional art forms for imagined cultures, e.g. how a tribe might celebrate the birth of a new queen; or an imagined **folk-form** may be used as a way of introducing a new drama; or the group may work within an existing **folk-form** in order to discover the culture it represents, or to understand the experiences described in the **folk-form**.
Cultural connections	Myths; legends; shanties; folk songs; traditional dances; rock and roll; jive and bop; YouTube phenomena; social media fads, and so on.
Learning opportunities	Working within structure and limitations of traditional form; empathising and identifying with alien historical and cultural contexts through the involvement with appropriate art forms; exploring class and culture through vernacular and minority forms.

Examples

1   A group of scientists are living through an experiment to see how pre-industrialised people survived in wilderness conditions. Rather than recording their adventures and researches in diaries and digital form, they decide to enact them through **folk-forms** they imagine the tribe would have used to record and express significant events in their lives.

2   A devising ensemble is working on themes of migration by looking at the images and narrative in Shaun Tan's *The Arrival* (Lothian Books, 2006). In one image a lonely migrant looks into his suitcase and sees his family at home eating without him. The ensemble imagine a group of migrants living together in a hostel who form a Suitcase Theatre (i.e. no props or costumes beyond those that can be easily carried) to perform their stories of loss and longing for families and homelands. These stories are performed in a variety of **folk-forms** appropriate to each migrant's home culture.

Forum-theatre

Description	A situation (chosen by the group to illuminate a topic or experience relevant to the drama) is enacted by a small group while the others observe. Both the actors and the observers have the right to stop the action whenever they feel it is losing direction, or if they need help, or if the drama loses authenticity. Observers may step in and take over roles or add to them. Sometimes this convention is mediated by the organiser or another group member acting as external referee or mediator – a role often called the 'Joker' – with the power to freeze the action and ask the audience members for suggestions.
Cultural connections	Giving/receiving advice; multi-dialogue options in games; educational 'choice gaming'.
Learning opportunities	Selecting appropriate situations; helping and advising each other; paying close attention to what is being performed; discussing and negotiating differing interpretations; different attitudes to the event worked through in action.

Examples

1   A group have been looking at the story of family in which the husband is in despair after losing his job. Such is his sense of powerlessness that he simply sits around all day doing nothing.

The group decide to explore ways in which the community could support the husband. With this in mind, they create a scenario designed to help the husband cope by exploring a meeting in which a community volunteer talks to the husband to encourage/ help him find some kind of purpose in the everyday, to tackle something positive around the home or to look beyond his own situation and volunteer himself.

One participant takes the role of the volunteer and another the role of the husband. When either volunteer, in their respective roles, run out of ideas and approaches, the 'Joker' freezes the action and asks audience members for their input. The observers may suggest an adjustment in tone and approach or a change in the type of advice given, or even take over the playing of either role.

2   A group of factory workers, whose workplace is threatened with closure, go to a government office to ask for aid to keep some employment in their community. The official explains that there is limited cash available and that they will need to make out a case for being a priority. Observers help to strengthen arguments and make points.

Genre switch

Description	Working in small groups, participants choose and perform dramatic situations or text extracts, either rotating through different genres (e.g. romcom, melodrama, pantomime, soap opera, western, cartoon, MTV video, science fiction, Bollywood movie) or developing a more detailed improvisation within a selected form.
	Where possible the original structure of and character relationships within the chosen material should still be evident and changes made should showcase the selected genre.
Cultural connections	Immediate experience of examples such as those given above.
Learning opportunities	Fun; spontaneity and group give and take; deeper understanding of the shape and dynamic of the selected material; developing confidence in expressive performance.

Examples

1   In a rehearsal of the final act of Anton Chekov's *Three Sisters* (Digireads.com, 2009), the actors are asked to perform the essence of the act in the style of a 1920s Sergei Eisenstein silent movie (e.g. *Strike*, *Battleship Potemkin* and *October*).

2   The opening scene of William Shakespeare's *Hamlet* from Barnardo's line:

> Who's there?

to Marcellus' line:

> LET'S do't, I pray, and I this morning know
> Where we shall find him most conveniently.

is played out firstly as a Hammer Horror film and then as a melodrama.

3   An edited version of Act 1, Scene 1 of William Shakespeare's *Othello* is broken down into four parts and each part taken on by a sub-group. Their task is to perform it as a very comic **Commedia dell'arte** scene using thrust stage, **masks** and props for the main characters. The group consider how this comic treatment brings out the **Commedia dell'arte** types that Shakespeare builds on and what the impact is on their understanding of Brabantio.

Elaboration

This convention could be embellished by using Grommelot – the 'babble-speak' of **Commedia dell'arte**.

Gestus

Description	In an otherwise realistic scene participants are asked to include an action, gesture or other visible sign that is intended to stand for a social relationship between the characters. Since the action or sign is intended to reveal the social context, it should comment on and clearly show the true social relations between the characters. In addition, the action should contain a contradiction. For example, a servant makes a respectful bow to his master (*action*) and at the same time mutters an insult under his breath (*contradiction*). When presented, the **gestus** in the scene should stand out from those actions and signs that are to do with the immediate 'here-and-now' of the situation represented.
Cultural connections	Brecht for social/historical **gestus**; common device in both drama and film; text/subtext in human relationships; observing character traits in family and friends; motion capture technology; Xbox Kinect; PlayStation Move; MotionScan; Janimation.
Learning opportunities	Dialectical; critical awareness of the social implications of action; heightened collective experience.

Examples

1 In a play-building structure that follows a doomed marriage between unsuitable partners, participants devise a scene to show the circumstances in which the wedding rings were bought. As part of the scene the group must include a **gestus** that reveals the true relationship between the couple who otherwise appear in love and unaware of the problem that will eventually separate them. For example, the man holds the woman's wrist and forces the ring, which is obviously too small, onto her finger.

2 In a drama based on Angela Carter's retelling of the Little Red Riding Hood story from *The Bloody Chamber and Other Stories* (Vintage Classics, 1995), Little Red Riding Hood's widowed mother (**teacher-in-role**) argues with the group in collective role as Little Red Riding Hood. The mother initially treats her daughter as a young child who is too vulnerable to go alone into the woods, but finally relents and agrees to her going. As Little Red Riding Hood packs her basket, the mother reveals a hunting knife wrapped in a black shawl and says to her daughter: 'Here; take your father's hunting knife, don't cut yourself.'

Living newspaper

Description	This convention is best used on material drawn from current issues – issues of the kind that participants might encounter on news feeds, blogs, YouTube or in the press – and which can be brought to life on the stage. The style of performance should be presentational and intended to shatter the traditional notion of the fourth wall that separates representational actors and audience in naturalistic theatre.
Cultural connections	Pop videos; hashtag activism; digital campaigning; satirical radio and TV programmes.
Learning opportunities	Choosing and expressing personal analysis and critique of current events; selecting content; finding appropriate form for the expression of a critical attitude towards aspects of society and world events.

Example

1 Such is the topicality required of the **living newspaper** that any current example would have dated by the time it is published.

Our example takes, what was perhaps the Federal Theatre Project's (FTP) most popular **living newspaper**, *Power*, from 1937. The production sets out to dramatise the story of the development of the electricity generation and supply industry in the USA set against the struggle of ordinary people to control that industry. The production was developed from participants acting as a **living newspaper** staff mirroring that of an actual printed newspaper, with an editor-in-chief, reporters, copyreaders, and so on who gathered the research material as a rough collection of facts, statistics, newspaper headlines and stories, and anecdotes for the script. These 'journalists' were then paired with dramatists and together they began refining the material towards the creation of a script.

Power chronicled the history of electricity from its discovery to its impact on the drive for modernity and progress, and combined this narrative with the story of the ordinary consumer's search for sensibly priced electricity.

Against the backdrop of this struggle the play sets the 'little man' figure – a unifying character who represents the consumer, who appears throughout the play, asking questions out of curiosity and receiving explanations. This fictional average consumer, Angus K. Buttonkooper, is led through the detail and background of the problem, and as he learns of problems and possibilities, this clarifies issues for the audience.

The production style was deliberately broad with quick scene and set changes using two-dimensional hand-carried and projected scenery, abrupt blackouts and harsh spotlighting. As with other FTP **living newspapers**, *Power* relied on projections on scrims presenting themes and dates, statistics, headlines and maps, along with visual images such as photographs and animated shorts, while a loudspeaker as a virtual character was used to narrate and comment on the action. In terms of dramatic construction, much use was made of **Montage**, alternating quickly between scenes and voices to emphasise conflicting and contradictory viewpoints and to comment on the action.

While the owners of the private companies are heard as they accuse the government of unethical business practices and federal programmes such as the Tennessee Valley Authority of attempting to undercut and financially cripple the private sector, *Power* is very clear who the villains of the piece are. In scene after scene, consumers are seen to be cheated by inflated charges, fail to obtain adequate services or are offered access to a power supply only if they can bribe the private companies to expand into their area.

Power takes the position that all citizens have a human right to such a service, coming out strongly in favour of state intervention, while private business insists that access to electricity supply is a privilege. However, despite the stand that *Power* takes on the matter of state ownership, the play itself concludes before a decision is reached, ending with an unanswered question and a visual question mark on the final curtain. The question, 'What will the Supreme Court do?' announced from a loudspeaker, in reference to the other New Deal programmes that had already been deemed unconstitutional by the nation's highest court, suggests to the audience that this debate is carried on outside the theatre.

 # Masks

Description	These are sometimes seen as being useful solely for presentational work, but have rich potential for changing perspectives. There are a wide variety of **masks** – full, half, character, anonymous, and so on – that can be made economically.
Cultural connections	Fancy dress parties; dances; the desire to create fear, horror and laughter in a safe way; the need to be ridiculous and incongruous in familiar situations; **rituals** and **ceremonies** where the personalities of the protagonists are less significant than the attitudes they portray; make-up; avatars.
Learning opportunities	**Masks** create distance and alienation, exploration of the incongruous and the grotesque; enhancement of perception of **ritual**.

Examples

1 In a performance project, based on the growing plight of young, homeless people, the group use neutral half-masks for all authority roles as a way of symbolising the vast imbalance of power between the individual and the state.

2 A group are exploring the traditional Panchatantra tales from India as subject matter for a Celebration of Difference event. They decide upon a tale called 'The Little Mice and the Big Elephants'.

A group of mice set up their home near a great lake. Every day at dusk a herd of elephants visit the lake to drink its water. On their way to the lake, the elephants accidently crushed many of the mice under their huge feet. So the mice decided to ask the Elephant King for help. When King Mouse met King Elephant and he heard the problem, he readily agreed to change the route to the lake. King Mouse in return promised to help the elephants if ever they had a problem in the future.

Now not long afterwards some elephant hunters came and trapped many of the elephants in large, strong nets. As hard as the elephants struggled, they could not break free. King Elephant, who had not been trapped, racked his brains for a way to release his herd. Suddenly, he remembered the promise of the mice.

As soon as King Mouse heard of the problem, he took his entire group to rescue the herd. The mice set nibbled the nets until they began to come apart. Then the elephants broke free from the nets and escaped from the hunters. They were so grateful to the mice for their help that they became friends for ever.

The group design and make a series of animal masks and, using **physical theatre** techniques to create the elephants, devise a performance retelling the story.

Mimed activity

Description	This activity emphasises movement, actions and physical responses rather than dialogue or thoughts. It may include speech as an aid to enactment, encouraging a demonstration of behaviour rather than a description of it.
Cultural connections	Silent films; archive material; dance forms; dreams; charades; mime games; lip-syncing; documentaries with voice-over commentaries; crowds in the street, markets, football matches.
Learning opportunities	Busy, active convention; selecting movements to match action; removes pressure of dialogue; encourages gestures and body language; useful way of establishing a context, i.e. workers on a production line; may be stylised, accentuating movement through dance, emphasising underlying actions; impulsive/ aggressive responses can be controlled by slowing mime down.

Examples

1   A group working on the history of mining devise **mimed activities** to show aspects of a miner's life. These mimed sequences are prepared in the style of archive film clips to form the introduction to a TV programme. The film clips show miners cutting the coal face, visits from the tallyman, miners descending in the cage, and mourning after a disaster. All these clips are shown in real time. The clips are then enacted simultaneously in slow motion while a volunteer sings the traditional ballad *The Gresford Disaster*. The effect of the slow motion and the song is to draw attention to the significance of the actions and what they represent. The first two verses set the scene.

> You've heard of the Gresford disaster,
> Of the terrible price that was paid,
> Two hundred and forty-two colliers were lost,
> And three men of a rescue brigade.
>
> It occurred in the month of September;
> At three in the morning the pit
> Was racked by a violent explosion
> In the Dennis where gas lay so thick.

2   In a drama exploring issues around the migration of workers from the countryside to the town, participants in role as unemployed farm workers meet with a foreman. In order to prove their potential as employees they are taken through a mimed sequence of the physical activities that will be expected of them should they prove themselves suitable to be taken on.

Montage

Description	**Montage** juxtaposes form and content so as to distort or challenge a stereotypic or conventional view. Through the combination of disparate elements to form a united whole, it provokes a fresh look at material that may be stale and creates interesting contrasts between elements in the drama that would not naturally be brought together. The intention here is that by connecting dissimilar elements in this way shocks the viewer into new perceptions and understandings.
Cultural connections	Photographic and film montage; slideshows; 'Best of' videos; compilations; BuzzFeed streams; Reddit forums and debates; surrealist art; cartoons; fantasy comics; satirical drawings; posters; pop videos.
Learning opportunities	Reflection on and experimentation with the relationship between form and content; reconsideration of original, unquestioned interpretations of meanings through the shock of unusual or demanding combinations of form, or disparate elements of content.

Examples

1 Amy Hest's *When Jessie Came Across the Sea* (Walker Books, 1999) tells the story of a young girl who leaves Europe for the United States of America at the end of the 19th century. A group exploring the issues underpinning emigration split into three groups and begin creating a series of **still-images**. The first two groups create images based on life going on as usual in Jessie's homeland without her and life for Jessie aboard a sailing ship respectively. The third group create a series of images around arrival, Ellis Island and the following lines from Emma Lazarus' poem *The New Colossus* engraved on a tablet on the base of the Statue of Liberty:

> …Give me your tired, your poor,
> Your huddled masses yearning to breathe free,
> The wretched refuse of your teeming shore.
> Send these, the homeless, tempest-tossed to me,
> I lift my lamp beside the golden door!

All three groups create a timed **soundscape** as a backdrop to their images and work on morphing from one image into the next as their **soundscapes** play out. Where necessary the **soundscapes** are adjusted until they are all approximately of the same length.

Finally, the group work at **montaging** the three strands of their devising, playing certain sequences individually, creating overlaps between two sets of images and then all three sets, and also exchanging soundtracks. Their intention is to create a **montage** that in a compressed timescale gives an audience insight into the whirlpool of emotions, thoughts and aspirations felt on leaving one's home for the unknown.

> There is no sorrow worse than this sorrow
> the dumb grief of the exile
> among villages that have strange names
> among the new rocks.
> The shadows are not his home's shadows
> nor the tales his tales
> and even the sky is not the same
> nor the stars at night.

Iain Chrichton Smith's *There is no Sorrow* from *New Collected Poems* (Carcanet Poetry, 2011)

2   Other interesting examples of **montage** readily available on the Internet can be found in the work of Russian auteur Sergei Eisenstein's films, in particular *The Battleship Potemkin* (1925) and *Strike* (1924).

Physical theatre

Description	Drama and performance work in non-theatre spaces and places without the backup and support of the mechanics of theatre is inevitably a fast-moving activity where location and *mise en scène* is sketched rather than created naturalistically. Thus in many ways this theatre convention is the bedrock of much drama activity in non-theatre spaces.
	As a form it emphasises individual and collective movement and the physicality of the body in order to carry the narrative of the piece. Although it may have aspects of mime, the convention embraces dialogue. Either individually or in small groups, as required, participants create all the visual elements of a stage picture by physically assuming, as accurately as possible, the material shapes of any aspect of the necessary environment for a drama through the physical representation of creatures, characters and aspects of location, building these animate and inanimate features of the narrative through organised lifting and weight-bearing.
Cultural connections	A central mode of children's play where individuals become inanimate objects, animals, and so on; augmented and virtual reality; Google Glass; the physicality of sport and game-playing.
Learning opportunities	Provides a quick, fun and creative way of establishing context; frequently requires contact and support from other group members, thus nurturing sensitivity and trust; requires controlled physicality towards expressive performance.

Examples

1   Whilst exploring teen relationships with parents, the following scenario is suggested. A 15-year-old girl has stormed out of the house after a row with her mother/carer. During her absence, the mother goes to clean her room. She finds a 'prop' such as a message, letter, text or email, that causes her to fear for her daughter and what she imagines is happening to her. The group create the scene using actors to represent the furniture in the room, which speaks the girl's secrets, hopes and fears as the mother passes or cleans it. The rest of the group, using physical symbolism and dance, slowly form the nightmare that grows in the mother's imagination as she finds the 'prop'.

2   Jane Yolen's *Here There Be Dragons* (Harcourt, Brace & Co., 1993) is a collection of poems and stories about dragons. 'Great-Grandfather Dragon's Tale' tells of the coming of man

from the dragons' point of view. Using extracts from Yolen's text, participants perform this story, creating the dragons, the world of ice and fire and the eventual arrival of a new creature 'smaller than the least of the dragons'. No fire and smoke, no claws:

> But when he opened his mouth, the sounds of all beasts, both large and small, of the air and the sea and the sky came out. It was this gift of sound that would make him the new king.

Elaboration

See also Indian Kathakali, Chinese Jingju and Japanese Butoh, Noh and Kabuki theatre.

Play within a play

Description	Characters in a drama perform a clearly defined and signed performance event within the context of a wider dramatic fiction. This performance put on by characters as actors for other characters effects a consequent blurring of the division between actor and audience, which creates various levels of reality. Members of the onstage audience are freed by this convention to comment on the performance from their perspective, and operating as critics of the event provide an outside audience with a double perspective.
	This convention can be used within either a performance context or an in-role drama that will, in this latter case, require not only its performance but also its devising from a frame perspective.
Cultural connections	'Story within a story' as a general narrative convention in literature, film and TV; live streaming of people commenting on games as they play them: PewDiePie; reality TV tasks and challenges; *Gogglebox*.
Learning opportunities	Layering of roles; selecting and crafting meaning from a frame perspective; representing meanings through appropriate selection of form; shaping into logical sequence.

Examples

1   This metatheatrical convention is a long-established and popular form and examples abound, such as Jean Anouilh's *The Rehearsal*, Bertolt Brecht's *The Caucasian Chalk Circle*, Anton Chekhov's *The Seagull*, Jean Giraudoux's *Ondine*, Tom Stoppard's *Rosencrantz and Guildenstern Are Dead* and Tennessee Williams' *The Two-Character Play*. But perhaps most well known are those of William Shakespeare: *A Midsummer Night's Dream*, *Love's Labours Lost* and *Hamlet*.

The Mousetrap or *The Murder of Gonzago*, the **play within a play** in *Hamlet*, is set up by the Prince himself to provide a mirror to the murder of his father as related by the Ghost. Hamlet intends to use the play to confirm first the truth of the Ghost's story and second the guilt of Claudius. As he says, 'the play's the thing / wherein I'll catch the conscience of the King'.

2   Undertaking a project exploring the world-view and value systems of indigenous peoples, a group had become particularly interested in the Lakota, members of the family of the Great Sioux Nation of North America. Their explorations were informed by the following

quote by Luther Standing Bear, from his work *Land of the Spotted Eagle* (University of Nebraska Press, 1988, c.1933) in which he wrote of: 'the Lakota belief that man did not occupy a special place in the eyes of Wakan Tanka, the Grandfather of us all. I was only a part of everything that was called the world.'

Having created a Lakota encampment, the group explored the daily life of the Lakota with its emphasis on the belief that the spirits within the natural life of animals, plants, water, air, earth and humans are all bound together in mutual **harmony**. Having spent time living in the shoes of these people, they then split into four groups to create story plays for the people of the tribe based on traditional Lakota stories of the meadowlark, the coyote, the eagle and the white buffalo. These were presented during a participatory drama as part of a feast, with each group taking it in turns to perform and to watch the other's performance as the Lakota people.

Prepared roles

Description	Another individual, parent, student or older pupil is brought into the drama to play a role accurately and authentically, i.e. he/she never comes out of role. The organiser's task is to facilitate the group's meeting with this role, and to involve the group in exploring his/her lifestyle, problems, needs and challenges.
Cultural connections	Strangers; helping people in need; visitors to school; eccentrics in the community; meeting people from other cultures.
Learning opportunities	Using someone who strongly represents another lifestyle is a very powerful visual aid for work; provides own focus and tension; makes immediate emotional and intellectual demands on the group, i.e. the role will not go away and come back later; shifts emphasis onto a weighing of human relationships.

Examples

1   The organiser wants to start a project by appealing to young people's 'natural' wish to help those in trouble. The group are framed as medical/social workers by the organiser in the role of a doctor (**teacher-in-role**), who introduces them to a young woman (another person in a prepared role) sitting hunched up, distressed, nervous and clutching something in her hand. The doctor explains that the woman has been found sitting by the canal and has been brought in, but that he has been unable to communicate with her. Can they help?

2   A group of 14-year-olds prepare, in great detail, to represent a wandering, hungry tribe of hunter-gatherers. The 'tribe' are taken to a local special needs school, where they are met by a group of children who look after them and eventually join their tribe. The organiser takes the role of a landowner who wants the tribe off his estate.

Readers' theatre

Description	This convention allows the dramatic presentation of material not originally written for performance. Poems (dramatic and lyric), narrative fiction, non-dramatic literature, novels and so on may all be used and should be chosen because of their relationship to a central theme.
	The performers in **readers' theatre** are usually stationary, seated on boxes, stools or chairs, and they make no secret of the fact that they use manuscripts either held in their hands or placed on lecterns in front of them. Readers do not establish eye contact with one another but instead maintain offstage focus. Employing vivid vocal and physical clues, they invite an audience to see and hear characters in imagined scenes taking place in front of them in the midst of the audience.
Cultural connections	Anthologies of poems, short stories, essays, short films; microblogging platforms and social networking websites such as Pinterest, Gentlemint and Tumblr.
Learning opportunities	Reflection on, and analysis of, a broad range of research materials; selection and sequencing of ideas for best effect; the translation of the written word into an effective theatrical experience.

Example

1   A theatre group rehearsing a production of Peter Whelan's play *The Accrington Pals* – which focuses on the first years of the 1914–18 war and culminates with the Battle of the Somme in 1916 – had researched background material around events both leading up to and depicted in the play. The actors had accumulated a broad range of resources and decided that much of the material was so moving that it had performance possibilities in its own right. The group therefore decided to devise and stage a **readers' theatre** performance as a short lunchtime event and precursor to their evening production.

These lines from Show of Hands' song 'The Padre', taken from their *Centenary* album, were chosen to bookend the performance:

> Each night I pray in my poor fashion
> God bless the Tommy, God bless the Hun
> And all the privates and their captains
> And all their widows and all their sons
> And the devout, the non-believers
> And the survivors and all the slain

That all who witnessed such destruction
May never witness the like again.

The performance itself drew on first-hand testimonies from civilians on the home front, in both the UK and Germany, and those of soldiers fighting on both sides, and also from diary accounts, poems and songs, battalion orders and official reports, and everyday documents such as weather and newspaper reports and so on.

Re-enactment

Description	An event that is known, or has previously occurred, is **re-enacted** in order to reveal what might have happened, or in order to discover its social dynamics and tensions. There is an emphasis on accuracy of detail and authenticity. This may be a whole-group **re-enactment**, or small-group presentation.
Cultural connections	Reconstructions of crimes; historical dramas; closed-circuit TV; film taken by spies.
Learning opportunities	Attention to detail, researching relevant data; reflecting on the event; analysing the social interactions that take place.

Examples

1 A group working on the migration of pioneers across America in the days of the wagon trains **re-enact** the burial of a small baby who dies on the journey. The group bring themselves into a 'photo' taken at the moment of leaving the burial; they arrange themselves so as to represent the different attitudes towards infant mortality and the various attitudes of the people sharing the journey. Their work is based on research into the nature of the journey and the kinds of people who undertook the venture.

2 Detectives investigating a murder **re-enact** what they think might have happened, based on their knowledge of the victim, her background, the position she was found in and information collected since the crime.

Reminiscence theatre

Description	**Reminiscence theatre** involves the creation of theatre by or for seniors. It is based in no small measure on the view that seniors in some modern-day societies are a marginalised and often forgotten group.
	The theatre created may be performed by seniors themselves, by seniors and younger people together or by younger people alone.
	The content of the work is the life experience of older people, but this does not mean that the work is trapped in the past. Recollection may drive the process, but equally there is a concern in the work for the here and now. Some reminiscence may generate **verbatim theatre** to a greater or lesser degree. Equally, this may not be the case as while work may grow out of interview-based reminiscence, the material is seen as content to be mined for its universal meaning for both young and old alike. Consequently, individual reminiscences may be sampled, linked with others, common themes identified and the work shaped for a variety of communities of interest.
	It would seem that most importantly **reminiscence theatre** is about communities recovering the legacy of the elderly and reintegrating both the seniors themselves and the wisdom gained from their experiences back into society.
Cultural connections	Cultures in which the contribution of seniors is respected; situations where life experience is seen as a community resource; the wisdom of age; the power of memory, recollection and remembrance.
Learning opportunities	Learning from the past to inform the present and the future; recognising the power of the cultural wisdom held by seniors; developing confidence in the structuring of material, the process of selectivity and assurance in expressive performance.

Examples

1   A group of inner-city seniors, concerned about the gentrification of their neighbourhood by property developers, devise a play that contrasts their neighbourhood then and now.

The work is performed in local community venues to a general audience and for other seniors in drop-in lunch clubs and residential care.

2   In a community recently devastated by floods and with a history of such disasters, an inter-generational theatre project brings together professional actors, seniors and young people to explore the community's response over time and to create a piece of campaigning theatre aimed at securing new flood defences.

3   Elders of African descent work with young immigrants, sharing and contrasting their life stories and experiences. They move on to perform short scenes based on their collective experiences at the young people's school, with the elders performing the young people's stories and vice versa.

4   Young people interview seniors at a local lunch club. They link this material with reminiscences collected from further interviews with members of their extended family and return to share short performance pieces at the lunch club. They gain feedback on their work from talking with the seniors after this initial performance work and return to the drama studio to refine and extend their material. Once they are satisfied with the shape of their work, they return to share it at the lunch club again, and then take their performance to other senior centres in the immediate area.

 # Revue

Description	A **revue** is a sequence of scenes or performance elements, which may or may not be loosely linked, providing an overview of social conditions and human attitudes. This overview is provided without the need to relate the parts selected to a unified plot or storyline and without the need to determine a common performance style or form.
Cultural connections	Stand-up and online comedians; GIFs; memes; Vines; Snapchat; TV programmes, perhaps most famously *Monty Python*.
Learning opportunities	Gaining a sense of the broad sweep of events, their relationship to individuals and the social framework that has given rise to them.

Examples

1 Interested in supporting Oxfam's long-term campaign against world poverty, a group select a range of sources – personal testimony, jokes, statistics, song, poetry and news report – and create a series of dramatic explorations of these sources with transitional links provided through the dramatised use of the following headings, taken from Oxfam's statement of Basic Rights:

Every person has a Basic Right to:

Enough to eat
A livelihood
An education
A safe environment
Equality of opportunity
Clean water
A home
Health care
Protection from violence
A say in their future

2 As a way of sharing their understanding of the cultural diversity of their neighbourhood, a group devise a celebration of these differences using representative multicultural extracts from **rituals**, stories, **folk-forms**, and so on.

 # Ritual

Description	**Ritual** is a stylised enactment bound by traditional rules and codes, is usually repetitive and requires individuals to submit to a group culture or ethic through their participation.
Cultural connections	Fraternity and sorority initiation; university society initiation; giving witness in court; elections; oath-taking; received images of tribal societies.
Learning opportunities	Group ideology or ethic symbolised and revealed through ritual activity ('What does this initiation tell us about the group we're joining?'); controlled and highly structured activity requiring reflective attitude; challenging individuals within an easily followed structure.

Examples

1 A detailed environmental project was organised around sub-groups exploring the question of global warming with each group taking a different area of the planet as their focus. Each sub-group was given the task of reporting back their findings to the whole group using any appropriate drama form. The group who taken the Arctic and the Inuit as their group focus became particularly concerned with the possible impact of rising temperatures on Arctic sea ice and the potential damage this would cause to the Arctic ecosystem.

The great white polar bear became totemic for the group, as much as it was for the Inuit. Thus the group decided to present a **chamber theatre** production of an Inuit legend called 'The Woman and her Bear' – a version of which can be found in Lydia Dabcovich's *The Polar Bear Son: An Inuit Tale* (Houghton Mifflin, 1999).

As the story goes a lonely woman with no family of her own adopted a tiny, orphan polar bear. She named him Kunikdjuag, or 'my son' (Kunik for short) and shared her little food with him. He grew into a fine hunter and always brought food back for his 'mother'. So skilled was Kunik that the men of the village became jealous and decided to kill him. A young boy heard the men planning and warned Kunik's mother who, though her heart was breaking, sent her son away.

After many days grieving, the woman decided to search for her son, and after walking and walking eventually they met. Immediately Kunik ran to fetch her food, and from that day on never again would his mother feel hunger. And, in time, the men of the village came to understand that the love between the mother and her son was both real and true, and they came to talk of it with awe and pride.

As part of their storytelling the drama group enacted a **ritual**, mimetic dance impersonating the polar bear, as Inuit shamans have done for centuries.

2 A group of space travellers have been marooned on a planet for many years. Each day they gather to remind one another of some idea or custom from Earth that they must remember if they are to remain a civilised community. Events on the planet begin to challenge their **ritual**: 'To what extent are moral codes modified by environment and the need to survive?'

Role-reversal

Description	Roles are reversed as part of the action of the drama. This can take place as a play-within-a-play, where a group demonstrate to each other how they think another group or role will react, e.g. bank robbers behaving as they think guards will behave; mutinous crew demonstrating how they think the captain will respond to their demands. But equally, **role-reversal** can be set up as pair or small-group work, with the exchange of roles controlled by the organiser.
Cultural connections	Mimicry; imitation; conversation-in-your-head; speculating about other people's reactions; copying parents, teachers, police, and so on.
Learning opportunities	Actively exploring demands and tensions presented by a future situation; way of demonstrating hypotheses about human behaviour and reactions; preparation for demanding situations; means of reflecting on problems and ways of dealing with them.

Examples

1   In a drama concerned with the morality of Western advertising in the developing world, the group are working as a sales team for powdered baby milk. In order to fix and clarify the issues involved, the group work in pairs, one as a Nigerian housewife, the other as a salesperson. At a given signal from the organiser and at suitably difficult moments in the sales pitch, the pairs swap roles and attempt to continue the improvisation without pause, thus experiencing the encounter from both standpoints.

2   As part of their work on the theme of gender equality and exploring the limitations of stereotyping, a group of male astronauts demonstrate how they think women would be unable to handle their work. In response, a group of female astronauts demonstrate that they would not want to go into space with a sexist man by mimicking the way they think such a person would interfere with their work.

Shape-shifting

Description	The 'outer' or 'realistic' shape of one or more characters is contrasted with figures that represent the 'inner dance' or shape of the spirit/heart at that moment in the drama. The realistic figures are frozen while volunteers pair up with them. In silence the group are invited to take turns in moulding and shaping the volunteers. When this has been done, the volunteers silently choose the most appropriate shape and take position on the organiser's signal. The realistic figures move aside so that we are left with the images of the 'spirit'. Although this convention can also be used in a similar fashion to **alter ego**, it is perhaps better suited to reinforcing the emotional undercurrents of a dramatic moment through the juxtaposition of metaphorical images with action and dialogue.
Cultural connections	Shadows; dance forms; silent films; dreams; body mapping; Xbox Kinect; Playstation Move; Oldify and other face distortion apps.
Learning opportunities	Devising the images requires critical analysis of role; finding form to concretise affective response; enhancing audience perception of the emotional life of the character.

Examples

1 In a workshop exploration of Bertolt Brecht's *The Caucasian Chalk Circle* (Penguin Modern Classics, 2007) participants work in groups to enact the sequence from Scene 6 of the play in which Azdak tests Grusha and the Governor's Wife by asking them who will physically wrest the child Michael from the chalk circle. Each player is paired with a **shape-shifter**.

2 In Brecht's Play *Life of Galileo* (Penguin Books, 2008) Brecht chooses not to show the audience the scene between the Inquisition and Galileo in which he actually recants his views. Instead he gives us Scene 12 in which the Pope and the Inquisitor discuss their approach to Galileo.

> THE INQUISITOR: Practically speaking one wouldn't have to push it very far with him. He is a man of the flesh. He would give in immediately.

Scene 13, after he has recanted, has the stage direction: *Galileo has entered, so completely changed by his trial as to be almost unrecognisable.*

Actors rehearsing a production of the play decide to improvise this missing scene and to use **shape-shifters** for each of the principals. Throughout the improvisation these additional actors **'shape-shift'** the characters to explore and indicate their emotions and fears.

Small-group play-making

Description	Small groups plan, prepare and present improvisations as a means of telling a story, representing a hypothesis or to demonstrate alternative views/courses of action. The improvisations express existing understanding of a situation or experience.
Cultural connections	Sketches; improvisations, TV drama; plays done at school, in youth clubs, for families and friends; assemblies; collaborative online channels, e.g. StampyLongHead; Machinima; group Vines.
Learning opportunities	Sequencing of ideas; selection of content; characterisation; devising dialogue and events; performance skills; developing confidence in expressive performance.

Examples

1   As an introduction to work on the treatment of young offenders, the groups are asked to improvise scenes that show the various crimes that we associate with young offenders. The groups are asked to prepare carefully at least one character whose life can then be more fully explored in the subsequent drama work. These initial plays may demonstrate a certain amount of stereotyping and cliché – much of the work that follows will therefore be to do with challenging the views and ideas expressed at this stage.

2   The group are exploring the story of Yeh-Shen, a Chinese Cinderella story. In brief, the story tells how Yeh-Shen's only friend is a fish who is killed by her stepmother. When she discovers this, an old man appears to comfort her and tells her that the bones of the fish will grant her wishes. Her first wish is to go to the King's ball where she loses her golden slipper. Eventually the King finds her and marries her, but her stepmother and sister are returned to their village to live in a cave. During the drama, small groups improvise scenes with the following characters and dilemmas:

- Having discovered that her fish is dead, Yeh-Shen is crying in the kitchen, being comforted by the cook and maid, but she vows to have her revenge. The Old Man arrives with the news that she may wish on its bones. What will she do next?

- The King wishes to find the person who owns the golden slippers. His three advisors have to come up with a plan. The King is initially convinced that there is little point looking in a poor neighbourhood when obviously the wearer of the shoes would be from a noble background.

- Yeh-Shen's mother has been banished back to the village and is joining other women who are washing at the river. What will the women say/do? Does she try and hold on to her status? After all, Yeh-Shen is now Queen.

- Yeh-Shen is now Queen and meets with the King and his advisors. The King wishes to use the bones to make wishes for himself. How does Yeh-Shen respond?

Soundscape

Description	Sound, song, words and phrases, either pre-recorded or performed live, are used impressionistically to create the mood and atmosphere of a character's lived experience, e.g. How does it feel to be …? In this convention the group are encouraged to think of the **soundscape** as having a musical shape to it and to weave the various words, statements and sounds together, orchestrating them as precisely as possible (cf. **soundtracking**).
Cultural connections	Film soundtracks; radio broadcasts; binaural headphones and microphones; ASMR communities; relaxing videos online.
Learning opportunities	Creating the **soundscape** requires reflection on, and analysis of, both character and situation; selecting ideas and sequencing for best effect; finding form for affective responses to work in progress.

Example

1   Early chroniclers tell a strange story about some elfin children – a boy and a girl – who were found near the village of Wolf-pits in Suffolk at the beginning of the 12th century. They were like ordinary people in size and appearance except that they were green all over. Some country folk found them, bewildered and afraid, at the mouth of a deep cave. They spoke an unknown language and did not seem to understand anything that was said to them, so the peasants took them to a knight, Sir Richard de Calne, who had a castle at Wikes.

A group had read this traditional story of 'The Green Children' and were intrigued by the fact that the children had been drawn to this world from their own by the chiming of distant bells. Never having heard this sound before, the children followed it on and on until suddenly they turned a corner and came into the full light of the sun.

To begin their exploration of the story, the group created the **soundscape** that both first enticed the children on their journey and then greeted them on their arrival. The sweet sound of bells builds into the confusion and babble of inexplicable talk amid strange surroundings as they are taken to Sir Richard. The emphasis in this activity was to accent the children's perspective on journeying and to mirror their felt experience of its novelty and alien qualities.

Elaboration

Usefully called dreamscape, this is a convention akin to **soundscape**, but the sounds and words are focused on dream images, sounds, words and word phrases. Statements and sounds are orchestrated and will overlap at times. A volunteer may conduct and orchestrate the dreamscape.

TV times

Description	Action is presented as if controlled by TV or digital remote. The activity can be momentarily paused and held in freeze-frame – where a sequence of still pictures is created, representing an actual event broken down into its constituent parts. It can then be rewound and rerun. Additionally, small-group improvisations can be brought to life and sampled by 'channel-surfing', using an imaginary TV remote.
Cultural connections	A part of the daily **ritual**; Vimeo; Now TV; live streaming; controlling live broadcasts; YouTube; Netflix.
Learning opportunities	The various possibilities covered by this convention slow down the speed of real life and, by concentration on essentials, underscore moments of significant decision-making on the part of the original participants, whose actions are replicated in the dramatic fiction.

Examples

1   A group exploring the role of social protest in democratic society are examining the lives of 'ordinary' people whose protests gained popular support leading to social change, e.g. Gandhi, Benny Rothman (the Kinder Scout trespass) and Rosa Parkes (the Alabama bus boycott). The work on Rosa Parkes comes from a first-hand account that describes the day she left work in a clothing factory, caught a racially segregated bus and refused to give up her seat to a white man. She was arrested and the incident led to the great bus boycott that gave birth to Martin Luther King's inspirational 'I have a dream' speech.

In order to comprehend the pressures on Rosa at the point where she refused to obey, and to attempt to understand why her decision was made on that particular day, the group first construct the bus. Then, in an attempt to find the experience of being there that day, they pause, slow, rewind and rerun key moments of the action.

2   A group are working in the style of a selected range of everyday TV cartoons and soaps in order to better understand the media representation of family life. A **montage** of the group's sharing of their work is both created and controlled by use of a TV remote. Pointing the remote signals the start of each improvisation, which can then be stopped, overlaid with a new improvisation and returned to as appropriate.

Verbatim theatre

Description	**Verbatim theatre** is essentially a form of **documentary theatre** in which the performed text is generated from interviews with actual people. Whereas **documentary theatre** encompasses a broad range of primary and secondary sources, **verbatim theatre** is based upon the actual words spoken by the people interviewed. However, the form is not closed, and like all conventions is adaptable in the light of both intention and purpose.
	Consequently, **verbatim theatre** may well include imagined scenes and dialogue and reported speech in addition to direct personal reminiscence.
Cultural connections	Recalling times past; telling stories and sharing experiences.
Learning opportunities	Interview skills; arouses curiosity and interest; selectivity; finding appropriate form for the expression of selected content.

Example

1   In an inter-generational **reminiscence theatre** project actors interviewed seniors for their memories of the Second World War. Finding three Holocaust survivors in their interview groups, they decided to create a specific remembrance tribute entitled *Six Million and One,* utilising several sequences of verbatim testimony.

Recent professional productions of **verbatim theatre** projects for which scripts are available include: *The Laramie Project* and *The Laramie Project: Ten Years Later* by Moises Kaufman *et al.*, *My Name is Rachel Corrie* by Alan Rickman and Katharine Viner, and *The Permanent Way* by David Hare.

Elaboration

Variations on the form include testimonial theatre, in which a writer works with an individual to tell their personal story, and tribunal theatre, which is created from edited courtroom records.

D. Reflective action

Are you moved?	Narration
Builders of bridges	Postbox
Character box	Power line
Choral speak	Space between
Empathy knots	Spectrum of difference
Finger ballet	Taking sides
Gestalt	This way/that way
Gifting	Thought shower
Giving witness	Thought-tracking
Group sculpture	Voices in the head
Harmony	Wall of China
If I were you …	Walls have ears
Marking the moment	Window on the world
Moment of truth	

Uses

These conventions are used when there is a need to stand aside from the action and to take stock of the meanings or issues that are emerging, or as a means of reviewing and commenting on the action. They provide a way for the group to articulate what characters are thinking or to give a 'psychological commentary' affording insight into the physical action. The conventions provide the same opportunity as 'soliloquy' and 'reported speech' in lyric theatre.

Cultural origins

They are drawn from theatre, film and radio conventions where the pace of the action is broken or interrupted in order to let a psychological perspective through. There tends to be a slower than natural use of time and a deliberate use of space and objects to create a reflective atmosphere.

Level of demand

Many of the conventions require personal commitment and a level of seriousness and sensitivity that can be difficult for some participants to sustain. Reflective language and action depend on being able to abstract and communicate subjective responses to the drama. Some of the conventions require complex agreements, e.g. where spectators may be offering the thoughts of the actors as the actors portray the physical action.

Are you moved?

Description	This convention requires group members to make concrete their analysis of the world-view of a character. Group members are asked to consider the correlation between the values of a character and their own by physically positioning themselves in relation to their understanding of what motivates the character.
	They do this by focusing on a particular character and placing them at the centre of an imaginary target on the floor. An object, or actor, is placed in the target to represent the character.
	Next, the group determine the defining idea that they wish to analyse and position themselves around the character, closely or at a distance depending on their personal response to their understanding of the world-view of that character.
	This activity may not start with consensus, although consensus is likely to emerge. Its purpose is to see differences of opinion and encourage them to be explored and debated.
	Importantly, through this convention the group are not being asked to make an empathetic choice of character as with **taking sides**, but rather a choice based on ideas and not personalities.
Cultural connections	Support for team games; following and supporting ideas and causes on the Internet; blogs; documentaries and reality shows.
Learning opportunities	'Concretising' understandings of human values, principles and defining self-beliefs; choosing and expressing personal analysis; slowing action to provide reflective opportunities.

Example

1   During their study of William Shakespeare's *Henry V*, the organiser makes an installation of a cloak, crown and sword to represent Henry V. At various intervals, the organiser asks the group to physically position themselves in relation to the installation according to how close or far away they feel they are from Henry and what he believes about kingship/leadership. This is initially done before the exploration begins to assess preconceptions that the group might hold with regard to the iconic status of Henry V. The convention is repeated after working on Henry's 'Once more unto the breach' speech during the siege of Harfleur; after his speech to the governor of Harfleur, in which he threatens to massacre the women and children in the town; after his meeting with ordinary soldiers on the eve of Agincourt; and finally when he gives the order to cut the throats of the prisoners.

The group reflect on the various positions they have taken at different stages of the play and the complexities and ambiguities displayed in Henry's character.

Builders of bridges

Description	The members of a group are asked to physically represent the building blocks of a bridge linking estranged characters or factions in a drama. As each member of the group takes their place, they link hands and name aloud the particular personal qualities, e.g. tolerance, love, compassion, that they feel most necessary to improving or sustaining connections in the personal circumstances of the drama.
Cultural connections	Physical bridges as the heart of community; figure of speech.
Learning opportunities	Identification of the elements of conflict; reflection and analysis leading to an understanding of the potential for connections between people; 'concretising' understandings in action; combining analysis with affective response.

Examples

1 A group were looking at the work of international aid agencies and came across a real-life story that intrigued them, centred on an ActionAid project in Northern Burma run by Sao Noi Tun Naing.

   Sao Noi Tun Naing was placed in a Kanti-Shan village amid five Kachin villages. Religious differences meant that there was a long history of misunderstanding and tension between the two groups, as the Kanti-Shan are not only minorities in Burma but also Buddhist, while the Kachin are Christian.

   After discussion among the Kanti-Shan villagers, Sao Noi Tun Naing was able to gain agreement that something needed to be done about the bridge to the nearby market, which was damaged.

   However, as the bridge belonged to all the villages, it was necessary to consult with the other villages to gain their support. After meetings with representatives from the other villages, it was decided to take on the necessary work as a joint project, with each village providing labour for transporting building materials.

   The group were asked to construct the metaphorical bridge, which in addition to the physical bridge would need to forge strong links between these communities, naming the particular qualities that this situation would require for lasting unity.

2 Working on William Shakespeare's *Romeo and Juliet*, reach the point where both Romeo and Juliet are dead, and consider the nature of the metaphorical bridge of emotions and understandings that would need to be built between the Capulets and Montagues to end their feud once and for all.

Character box

Description	This convention works equally well with characters taken from both devised and scripted work. First, each group member is asked to choose a character from work in progress. Since this convention requires an individual and personal response, more than one person can select the same character. Next, participants are asked to begin a character analysis based on their chosen character's actions and dialogue and the things that others say about them. Then, as they identify particular characteristics, they are asked to think about them in terms of our five senses: sight, smell, touch, hearing and taste. The purpose here is to try to build up a more complete picture of the chosen character by gathering objects together for each of the five senses, so that these selections cumulatively highlight aspects of that character's life.
	Each participant then places their chosen items in a suitable box with a lid – such as a shoebox – and shares the story of and the reasons for their selection with the rest of the group.
	Where a scripted character has been selected, these choices can be linked back to and justified by specific lines of text from the play, and in devised work to specific encounters and actions.
Cultural connections	Personal effects; prized possessions; personal taste, influences and choices; Pinterest.
Learning opportunities	Analysing character traits; interpreting personality; attributing meanings and selecting appropriate tangible representation.

Examples

1. A group was rehearsing a production of Brecht and Hauptmann's *Happy End* – in which members of the Salvation Army and gangsters collide in Roaring Twenties Chicago – and each actor was asked to create a **character box** for the character they were playing. The actor playing Lieutenant Lilian Holiday – who falls into 'fairy-tale' love with Bill Cracker, the gangsters' boss – selected the following objects for her box:

(Sight)	A Salvation Army placard with the legend: Caring is Sharing
(Touch/feeling)	A dark brown homburg hat worn by the actor playing Bill Cracker
(Scent/smelling)	A bright red lipstick
(Sound/hearing)	A Salvation Army hymn sheet
(Taste/tasting)	A crust of stale bread.

When asked why the crust of bread she replied, 'Because the poor are always with us'.

2   Working on Shakespeare's *Romeo and Juliet*, a **character box** for Friar Lawrence might contain:

(Sight)	A letter to Romeo explaining his plan
(Touch/feeling)	A rosary
(Scent/smelling)	A cloth bag containing incense
(Sound/hearing)	A copy of the paternoster
(Taste/tasting)	A phial containing the remains of a sleeping potion.

Choral speak

Description	The group are asked to prepare a choral reading of a stimulus text using sound, song, repetition, emphasis and variety of voices as appropriate in order to highlight the essence of the material they are working on. The chosen text may be a playscript or otherwise. The construction of the **choral speak** should be crafted so as to provide a comment on, or further development of, the original text, rather than following any of the predetermined line breaks or previous allocation of lines to any particular characters.
Cultural connections	Children's nursery rhymes; chants; rhythmic poetry; choruses; street games; rap; ASMR choruses; online calls to prayer.
Learning opportunities	Requires the detailed and focused consideration of text and subtext; reflective analysis of meaning and selective focus on essential elements; the translation of a literary source into an effective aural experience.

Examples

1   The group are given copies of the following poem *Watching the Reapers* (C.E. 806) by the Chinese poet Bai Juyi (772–846):

> Tillers of the soil have few idle months;
> In the fifth month their toil is double-fold.
> A south-wind visits the fields at night:
> Suddenly the hill is covered with yellow corn.
> Wives and daughters shoulder baskets of rice;
> Youths and boys carry the flasks of wine.
> Following after they bring a wage of meat
> To the strong reapers toiling on the southern hill,
> Whose feet are burned by the hot earth they tread,
> Whose backs are scorched by flames of the shining sky.
>
> Tired they toil, caring nothing for the heat,
> Grudging the shortness of the long summer day.
> A poor woman follows at the reapers' side
> With an infant child carried close at her breast.
> With her right hand she gleans the fallen grain;
> On her left arm a broken basket hangs.
> And *I* to-day … by virtue of what right
> Have I never once tended field or tree?
> My government-pay is three hundred tons;
> At the year's end I have still grain in hand.

Thinking of this, secretly I grew ashamed;
And all day the thought lingered in my head.

Having discussed the poem and its use of language, the group is split in two on the basis of male and female voices, and the male voices are asked to prepare a **choral speak** reading of the poem from Bai Juyi's perspective, while the female voices are asked to prepare a reading from the point of view of the poor woman with the infant child. Both groups present individually and then together, playing with the overlap between the two readings.

2   The group are split into two and each sub-group is given one of the following speeches from William Shakespeare's *Measure for Measure* in their entirety (Claudio 131–150, Isabella 151–162). These speeches are taken from Act 3, Scene 1 and see the imprisoned Claudio pleading for his sister Isabella to save his life at the expense of her own honour. The sub-groups are asked to interpret their particular speech in **choral speak** and at the same time they must create a series of images evoked by the text. The objective is to try and fully develop the dark, angry, brooding imagery of the texts through voice and physical work. Finally, their performances are shared and the group are asked to use the convention **taking sides** to place themselves on a spectrum in terms of which character's viewpoint they most strongly support.

> **Claudio:** Ay, but to die, and go we know not where;
> To lie in cold obstruction and to rot;
> This sensible warm motion to become
> A kneaded clod; and the delighted spirit
> To bathe in fiery floods …
> Sweet sister, let me live …
>
> **Isabella:** O you beast!
> O faithless coward! O dishonest wretch!
> … Take my defiance!
> Die, perish! Might but my bending down
> Reprieve thee from thy fate, it should proceed:
> I'll pray a thousand prayers for thy death,
> No word to save thee.

Empathy knots

Description	At a critical point in a drama, three actors represent three key protagonists and stand in a triangle. The group are asked to consider which of the characters they have most empathy for and to stand behind their chosen character. If the drama has been a balanced exploration of the different points of view of the protagonists, then there should be group members behind each of the characters. Each group discusses the reasons for their choices. Their next task is to use the three actors to make an image that demonstrates their reasons to the other groups. They must use all three actors, but only them, and make the image without giving verbal instructions. The actors must all be physically linked. The challenge is to make an image and explanation that will be persuasive and change other participants' minds. As each image is made, the group responsible explain to the others how the image represents their understanding. When all three images are made, the whole group are given the chance to change their position if they have been moved in any way by another group's image or explanation. Reasons for moving/not moving are discussed with the whole group.
Cultural connections	Public art; advertising; persuasive argument; debates.
Learning opportunities	This convention helps the organiser to assess how balanced the group's exploration has been; participants have to consider the distinction between sympathy and empathy; discussion deepens reflection; a reminder that drama explores multiple perspectives and that different characters will be differently motivated.

Example

1 As part of a devising process exploring the theme of migration, the ensemble has worked with images from the opening of Shaun Tan's *The Arrival* (Lothian Books, 2006). These images include a depiction of a couple's last moment before the husband begins his journey of migration. Using improvisation and scripting, the ensemble present scenes based on this moment, focusing on how the scene builds to the climax of the couple's hands meeting on top of a closed suitcase. At the last minute, the organiser introduces the character of a child into the scene, who has been invisible and silent up to this point. What difference does the presence of the child make to the scene?

Three actors then make an **empathy knot** of the mother, father and child. The members of the devising ensemble then decide which of the characters they have most empathy for: the father who must go alone and create a new future for his family; the mother who must stay behind alone with her child or the child who will lose a father and cannot fully understand what is happening and why.

Finger ballet

Description	This convention is used as a reflective device to record a collective response, either as a direct participant in, or as an audience member for, a programme of drama work, individual session, performance and so on.
	Group members (six to eight is an ideal number, so larger groups are best split) lie on the floor in a circle with their heads to the centre. From this position they negotiate, plan and rehearse their joint responses to the event or events being analysed. Then using only their hands, they choreograph and rehearse a 'ballet of fingers', supported by whatever commentary and sound effects they consider necessary.
	Ideally, they then share this work with an audience drawn from other groups.
	Following this sharing, individuals (in groups or solo) use other conventions to explore further or challenge ideas, emotions and viewpoints they have either helped to create or seen presented.
Cultural connections	Dancing fingers; Charlie Chaplin's Table Ballet in *The Gold Rush* (The Roll Dance); YouTube videos.
Learning opportunities	Fun; negotiating and expressing a collective response; finding form for shared feelings and thoughts; 'concretising' reflection and analysis through expression; encouraging greater awareness of group work.

Examples

1   A group returning from their first experience of a live Shakespeare play **finger ballet** their initial responses.

2   Having spent a number of weeks devising a performance for a community action day, the group unwind by doing a **finger ballet** of their experience.

 Gestalt

Description	Following some initial work on a character, and prior to exploring that character's response to the core situation of a drama, the group split into pairs and devise dialogues that involve the protagonist and another character at a key moment in the protagonist's life. These can be taken from events real or imagined, past or future. The pair decide the most likely context and the most suitable role for the chosen moment by analysing the character's current disposition. It may well be that the core event is already known to the group – in which case future-based dialogues should take on implications of the event itself.
Cultural connections	Narrative device in literature; film conventions in which a number of actors are used to play the same character from youth to old age; multi-choice dialogue in video games, 'determine your own ending' narratives in apps and video games.
Learning opportunities	Requires extrapolation from detailed analysis of known character traits; provides opportunities for insight into the development of individual motivation, attitudes and values against the wider canvas of a variety of social interactions and perspectives; allows for appraisal of these factors and provides a more complex and rounded character for further exploration.

Example

1 Using William Still's *The Underground Railroad: Authentic Narratives and First-Hand Accounts* (Dover Publications, 2007) and Mary Kay Carson's *Which Way to Freedom?* (Sterling Children's Books, 2015) as sources for organiser and group, a drama had developed around a fictional Afro-American slave called Johnson, who was escaping to Toronto in Canada from the southern USA. Not actually a railroad, the Underground Railroad was a network of secret routes called 'lines' and safe houses called 'stations' supported by activists called 'conductors' and used by 19th-century slaves who were trying to escape to free states and Canada.

In each pair a participant played Johnson while their partner played a character drawn from the following: a suspicious officer of the law; a fellow slave on the run; a farmer; an abolitionist; a church leader; a conductor; a philanthropist and so on.

Finally, the sharing of these dialogues was orchestrated by the group organiser in role as Johnson moving from one pair to another and animating extracts from the work of each pair by standing silently with them.

 Gifting

Description	Members of the group are asked to 'gift' objects, talents, understandings and so on to a central character within the drama. These gifts can be either real items or drawn/described on slips of paper.
Cultural connections	Birthdays, name days, religious festivals; the careful matching of gift to recipient; web-based wishlists.
Learning opportunities	Considering and expressing personal analysis of human actions; creates strong affective resonance, empathy and reflection.

Examples

1   Actors working on a production of Jean Anouilh's *Antigone* (*Plays: One*, Berg, 2007) are given a copy of her last letter to Haemon, her betrothed and son of King Creon.

> Forgive me, my darling. You would all have been so happy except for Antigone.

They are asked to consider their responses to this text in the light of the fact that Creon has decided that Antigone must be punished for her disobedience, first in going against his explicit instructions and but then also as an example for the greater good of society. The group are then asked to create a **still-image** of Antigone standing awaiting her punishment in the mouth of the cave in which she is to be held.

Then working out of role as themselves, each member of the company is asked to 'gift' whatever they best feel will sustain her in the ordeal that is to come. Antigone receives the gifts in silence and without verbal response.

2   As a young girl packs to leave home for the first time, members of the group decide on an object, piece of advice or other gift that they would want her to take on her journey. Each item is chosen either because it will be useful or as a remembrance of home. Each group member publicly 'gifts' the item of their choice by both naming it and placing it formally in the girl's open suitcase.

Giving witness

Description	The organiser or other individual, gives a monologue purporting to be an objective account of events, but which in effect is a highly subjective retelling from the witness' point of view. The account is often charged with emotion – in the manner of oral history, evidence in court or inquiry.
Cultural connections	Oral histories; courtroom dramas in the media; hearing different accounts of the same event, e.g. own, teacher's, friend's; TV chat shows; monologues in media drama; memoirs; instant update Twitter feeds; live streaming; 24-hour news channels; opinion vlogs and blogs.
Learning opportunities	Combining information with affective response; identifying and establishing bias and prejudice; linking events to cultural and class environment; linking attitudes to events; shaping stories to match the teller.

Examples

1   In a study of Arthur Miller's *The Crucible* the group first hear a retelling of a witch hunt by the mother of the victim, and then by the father. Other individuals, more or less affected by the events, give their retelling as if it were some time later when they have had the chance to reflect. These monologues are then set against the way the same witnesses gave formal evidence at the 'witch's' trial. The group begin to concretise their opinions and understandings of the people involved from a discussion and analysis of the subjectivity contained in each account and what it tells them about the witness.

2   A group are looking at the effects of persecution and prejudice on a group of people who have been forced to flee their home planet in order to find freedom. Several generations later they participate in a 'remembrance moot', at which the youngest member of each family retells an oral history of the persecution as it has been passed down through the family 'lest they forget'.

Group sculpture

Description	An individual (or members from the group) models volunteers into a shape using as many members of the group and/or objects as necessary to reflect and encapsulate a particular aspect of the theme or issue under scrutiny. This activity usually produces images of a non-representational nature unlike **still-image**, which tends to favour literal representations.
Cultural connections	War memorials; monuments; funerary art; commemorative statues; art gallery exhibits; flash mobs; geo-cached sculptures; Storify.
Learning opportunities	The concrete visualisation of meaning through working 'as if' in monumental form can facilitate the group in the focus of their own collective interpretation of events.

Examples

1   In Lloyd Alexander's story *The King's Fountain* (Dutton, 1971) a powerful king wishes to build a fountain 'for the splendor of his kingdom and the glory of his name'. In role as 'fountain builders' the participants are asked to work physically on designs for the fountain. However, instead of getting to show these designs to the king as they expect, they meet an old man (organiser in role) who has come to try and persuade the king not to build the fountain. His story is that the fountain will cut off the water supply to the people of his village at the foot of the palace hill.

2   As part of a rehearsal room approach to William Shakespeare's *Henry V*, an ensemble are working with the ideas of thesis/ antithesis in the play and the idea of multiple perspectives. Participants begin by considering these words of Winston Churchill: 'We sleep soundly in our beds because rough men stand ready in the night to visit violence on those who would do us harm.' Using a **spectrum of difference** they position themselves according to how comfortable or uncomfortable they are with this statement. In small groups they are then asked to work in role as sculptors commissioned to produce monumental public sculptures, in each case with Winston Churchill's quote as the caption. The sculptures that they physically represent must attempt to illuminate the quotation from the perspective of the commissioning clients and reflect their values. The commissions are from: a veterans association; The World Peace Foundation; mothers of the fallen; an officer training academy.

 # Harmony

Description

This convention uses a Venn diagram to compare and contrast similarities and differences between the characters in a play or improvised drama. See the standard Venn diagram in Figure 4.

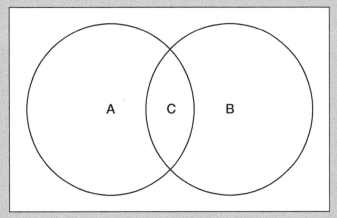

Figure 4   Compare similarities and differences between characters

Cultural connections

Communities of location; communities of interest; individual motivation set against social interaction.

Learning opportunities

Requires analysis of character traits and comparison between individuals; allows for discussion and appraisal of similarities and differences; provides concrete visualisation of meanings.

Example

1   A group working on Shakespeare's *Hamlet* creates a diagram that has four circles: a central one for Hamlet and three other circles, one each for Horatio, Laertes and Fortinbras (each of their circles overlaps the Hamlet circle a little.)

They place the characteristics and/or experiences that the characters have in common in the overlapping parts of the circles and discuss the differences in the larger parts of the circles.

To gather information about the characters, they reread the following scenes and their summaries:

Horatio: Act 3, Scene 2
Fortinbras: Act 4, Scene 4
Laertes: Act 4, Scene 7

The group work around the following quotation from Shakespeare's *Macbeth*:

> Such welcome and unwelcome things at once,
> 'Tis hard to reconcile.

Using this convention, the group decide which character traits are:

Welcome	Unwelcome
(Strengths)	(Faults)

The organiser then asks the group members to place words that describe Macbeth's welcome side (his strengths) and words that describe his unwelcome side (his faults). The group are then asked to consider which characteristics are both strengths and faults (ambition, being a good soldier, and so on) and therefore could be placed in the overlapping section.

If I were you …

Description	Sometimes called 'Conscience Alley', this convention is best used at a critical moment in a character's life when a decision must be made, or a dilemma, problem or choice must be faced.
	The character walks between two rows of group members, who provide an external commentary on how others see the character's situation by offering advice or comment as the character passes.
	The advice may be spoken by the participants as themselves or be offered in role as other characters; the advice may echo previous encounters within the drama and repeat lines of dialogue or words spoken earlier.
	The character listens to what is said but does not comment.
Cultural connections	Getting and receiving advice; helping people in need; advice vlogs from YouTube celebrities, lifestyle magazines, Facebook groups.
Learning opportunities	Analysing problems; helping and advising; slowing action to facilitate a more reflective stance; adding tension to imminent action; encouraging personal commitment and involvement.

Example

1 Starting from the stimulus of Nigel Gray's short story *The Party*, the group have been working on creating the streets of the locality in which the story unfolds. The story centres on a young boy, left at home all day by his mother, who decides to 'escape' from his 'prison' by climbing from a window into the street. The group have presented a series of short scenes showing local characters and their neighbourhood interrelationships and then used the convention of **a day in the life** to trace the pattern of events during the 24 hours leading up to the boy's decision to escape. They then complete this work by making a **still-image** of the child waiting in the doorway for the return of his mother, having failed to get back into the house. As the mother returns home towards the child, the group creates random groupings of neighbours who, in role, offer her advice on how best to deal with her son.

Elaboration

Crossroads Anthony Browne's picture storybook *The Tunnel* tells the story of sibling rivalry between Rose and her brother Jack. One of the book's images shows Jack crawling into a mysterious tunnel and leaving his sister behind. Having read the story to this point, the group are asked whether Rose follows or not. Then, working from the picture, the group arrange themselves so that they physically create a 'crossroads' where the decision must be made either to follow her brother into the unknown or to return home alone by the shortest route. A group member representing Rose is placed in the centre of the crossroads. The others give Rose guidance according to their place on the 'tunnel route' or on the 'short route home'.

Consequences Participants work in pairs to plan their input. Then the group create two parallel lines, each participant standing opposite their partner. As the protagonist walks between the parallel lines, one side offer their advice while the other side predict either the positive outcomes of taking the advice or the negative consequences of ignoring it.

Marking the moment

Description	This convention is used as a reflective device to 'mark' a position, place or a moment in the drama where a feeling is aroused, or an understanding of the issue occurs. As participants recollect that moment, they find physical form to represent their involvement at that time. Individuals (in groups or solo) use other conventions to express that feeling or understanding, or to explore further that position or moment.
Cultural connections	Poems, stories, pictures made in response to an important event – death, birthday, first kiss, being bullied, being let down, political event; commemorative photos, newspapers, memorials; civic sculptures; heroic verse, images, and so on; augmented reality showing the deeper significance of a place or object, geolocating media on digital maps.
Learning opportunities	Choosing and expressing own moment of focus in the drama; finding form for personal feelings and thoughts; 'concretising' reflection and analysis through expression; encouraging sensitive awareness of work.

Examples

1   As the culmination of several weeks' work exploring various aspects of the First World War, the group return to the position and place in the drama studio where they feel their own moment of new understanding occurred. Some 'mark' the trenches, some recruitment, some receiving letters, some learning new work skills, some a song. Individuals talk about the moment they have chosen and then represent their understandings and feelings through **still-images**, poems, improvisations or dance/mime.

2   As the culmination of a drama summer school, which has used a variety of spaces and venues on a university campus, the group move together around the site with individuals stopping as required to mark their personal moment. If others recognise this time and place, they join in as appropriate.

Moment of truth

Description	This is a means of resolving a drama, with reflective discussion on the events used as a basis for predicting a crucial final scene. Volunteers spontaneously act out this key moment of tension involving the main protagonists, with a view to establishing for the rest of the group what would happen in reality, rather than trying to create the moment to be entertaining or theatrical. The scene is played with different volunteers until the group are satisfied that the moment is truthful.
Cultural connections	*Cinéma-vérité*; documentary; watching sporting events; observation of real-life events; live streaming.
Learning opportunities	Allows participants to synthesise their understanding of the drama into action rather than discussion; tests out prejudices and assumptions in action; emphasises the effect of context on human actions; encourages a critical attitude towards the personal and social influences of class, gender, race and ability.

Examples

1 Having explored the problems of communication between a young woman and her father, the group create the moment at which the young woman has returned to the family home to remove her last personal possessions. Thinking that her father is out, the young woman leaves her key inside the doorway and then, having closed the front door, picks up the box of her possessions ready to leave, only to find her father coming in at the garden gate. The group use chairs to mark the path from the gate to the front door, and volunteers represent the father and the young woman, who walk towards one another. The rest of the group suggest their thoughts as they walk. The **moment of truth** is for the volunteers to decide and will answer the question: does she stay or will she go?

2 In a drama that explores a dilemma faced by a girl out shopping with her best friend, the friend steals a jersey and leaves the shop without her. The girl is stopped by a store detective, who asks for her friend's name and says she will be prosecuted as an accomplice if she does not give the name. The group try out alternatives as to what might happen when the two friends next meet.

 # Narration

Description	**Narration** can be used both in and outside the dramatic context. The organiser might provide a narrative link, atmosphere or commentary, initiate a drama, move the action on, create tension; or the participants might report back in story form, providing narrative to accompany action – 'we came to the river and saw that the bridge had been destroyed, so we …'.
Cultural connections	Key moments of children's play – 'I'm dead now, but when you come in I'll come alive and then we'll look for the others'; the need, on an adult level, to prepare for experiences by talking them through first, e.g. meetings when one wants to focus on the real issues; speculation videos; ASMR videos; how to videos.
Learning opportunities	Provides information in familiar form with affective resonance; gives shape and form to activity; arouses curiosity and interest; emphasises sense of atmosphere, place, and poetic description; involves feelings and moods; activity controlled by the content and form of the **narration**.

Examples

1   As part of a drama where a group of scientists are living as a primitive community, the scientists enact their day's research while one member of the group retells the events in narrative form.

2   A group of scientists are preparing to investigate a UFO that has landed in a remote place. As they walk slowly towards the object, the organiser uses **narration** to slow down the pace, create the atmosphere of the moment, suggest the scientists' attitudes and expectations, and build tension and belief into the context.

3   In a drama about an unhappy child, the group enact an event from the child's school life while alternative **narrations** are offered: the child's teacher's story, the child's story, the friend's story. Contrasts between viewpoints are highlighted in the differences between the various stories and between the stories and the action we see.

Elaboration

See also narrative performance traditions that use leader and chorus **narration** such as African 'orature'; Caribbean 'Crick Crack' storytelling; Japanese Kamishibai.

 # Postbox

Description	This convention asks participants to imagine a ritualised exchange of messages (short letters or postcards) between two characters. These characters need not necessarily inhabit the same time or space, or even be drawn from the same story. For an informed exchange there needs to have been previous intertextual exploration of both the characters.
Cultural connections	Getting and receiving advice; reaching out to others.
Learning opportunities	Each group member writes their own message in the imagined voice of one of the characters and it is then ritually posted for the other character to receive.

Examples

1   A group had been exploring in parallel the stories of the lives of Anne Frank and Rosa Parks. As the culminating activity the group were asked to write their own individual messages in the voice of their chosen character and then mail them.

2   A youth theatre group started their devising process by research and improvisation around Ray Bradbury's *Fahrenheit 451*, the science fiction novel that envisages a future in which firemen burn books – starting fires rather than putting them out. The central character Guy Montag, himself a fireman, patiently accepts his life until he is awakened by a meeting with a 17-year-old girl named Clarisse McClellan, who opens his eyes to the emptiness of his life. Following her death in a car accident, Montag becomes ever more dissatisfied, and begins to search for a solution in a stash of books that he has secreted from his own fires. Eventually, Montag becomes part of a network of book lovers who have each memorised a great work of literature or philosophy.

The group began to look out from the pages of the book to ask questions arising from their own lived experience. In other words, looking at the lives of 'those people', looking at their own lives and asking the questions:

1   What is the same?
2   What is different?
3   What needs to change?

These questions lead them to foreground in particular the struggle of Malala Yousafzai, whose fight to overcome ignorance and oppression has made her a worldwide ambassador for education. Using this convention the group imagined an exchange of letters between the real-life Malala and the fictional Montag.

Power line

Description	Group members stand characters from a drama in a line from -5 to +5 (see Figure 5) in terms of their relative status. The most powerful characters are positioned at or near plus 5, while less powerful characters occupy lower placings. The convention can be used at multiple points within an expanding drama in order to map changing power relationships and to provide a forum for discussion around cause and effect.
Cultural connections	The notion of a 'pecking order'; social stratification and social hierarchy; shifting power relationships and balances.
Learning opportunities	Defining and interrogating human relationships; appreciating the potential of power to be won and lost; 'concretising' understandings in action.

Figure 5   Spectrum of power

Example

1 Working on a production of Shakespeare's *King Lear*, the actors use a **power line** at a number of points in the play to delineate the shifting balance of power between Lear himself, his daughters and other characters in the play such as Edgar, Kent and Albany.

The group chart the heights of Lear's power from 'Come not between the dragon and his wrath' to the depths of his despair:

> Nor rain, wind, thunder, fire are my daughters.
> I tax not you, you elements, with unkindness.
> I never gave you kingdom, called you children.
> You owe me no subscription. Then let fall
> Your horrible pleasure. Here I stand your slave,
> A poor, infirm, weak, and despised old man.

Space between

Description	Participants arrange volunteers from the group, representing characters from the drama, so that the **space between** them symbolises how close their relationships currently are. Who feels close to whom? Who feels distant and estranged? Participants can also be asked to consider what change there might be in this space over time – will characters draw closer together or drift even farther apart? They can also try to put a name to the distance: love, respect, guilt, betrayal, anger, and so on (cf. **taking sides**).
Cultural connections	Family; relations; friends; Facebook friends; YouTube subscribers; Twitter followers; enemies; traitors; strangers; outsiders.
Learning opportunities	Analysis of role relationships; encourages critical awareness of the consequences of action; embodies and makes concrete emotional states.

Examples

1 Several sessions' work on Arthurian legend had given the group a sound basis in both character and storyline. **Space between** was used to consider the relationships between Arthur, Guinevere, Mordred and Lancelot before the participants moved on to explore events around the 'last battle'.

2 In a drama about a failing marriage, groups make formal wedding photos as a **still-image**. All the groups have developed their own storyline for their chosen characters and all are represented in the selected photo. Participants from other groups are invited to move the characters around, based on the scenes they have already seen from that story, so that the 'true' distance between them can be seen. They are then asked to name the distance as 'lack of trust' or 'fear of losing control', as appropriate. The participants reconsider how the distance may have changed after five or ten years. Finally, the group making the **still-image** are given the time taken for three hand claps to decide on and take positions that show their idea of the 'space between' the characters they represent.

3 In an exploration of the 8th-century poem *Watching the Reapers* by Bai Juyi, the group model the poor woman and her baby who follow the reapers, picking up whatever grains they miss, and the Tax Collector who observes this from a distance. The group make a circle of comments around each character that emphasises the social distance between them. The woman's circle is all the things that will prevent her from gaining the Tax Collector's status – poverty, gender, education, her baby – and the Tax Collector's circle is the things that prevent him ever becoming as poor as the woman – status, education, family ties.

Spectrum of difference

Description

This convention requires group members to place themselves physically on an imaginary line (see Figure 6) linking two alternatives, indicating their preference through their choice of position. An open mind is indicated through placing oneself centrally, while the closer one stands to a chosen alternative the stronger one's support. This convention allows participants to see the potential range of opinion within a group. With some groups it will be important to ask for the reasons for the choices made, but equally with other groups the convention can be set up so as to allow individuals the opportunity to make a statement without having to verbally defend their position.

e.g. WAR ——————————— Undecided ——————————— PEACE

Figure 6   Spectrum of opinion (1)

Cultural connections

Voting; show of hands; making a stand; Survey Monkey; online polls; Facebook polls; YouTube likes vs. dislikes.

Learning opportunities

Determining and expressing own values; 'concretising' understandings in action; combining information with affective response.

Examples

1   Participants exploring Ophelia's journey through William Shakespeare's *Hamlet* are asked to imagine a line running from one corner of the room to the other. At one end, is the point of strongest agreement at the other the point of strongest disagreement.

Participants are asked to move and position themselves along the axis, on the basis of the extent to which they agree/disagree with the following statements:

- 'In the world where murder holds sway there is no room for love'.
- Hamlet's love for Ophelia is simply a 'fashion' / 'sweet not lasting'.

This activity is first conducted in silence, without discussion. Once everyone is in place, the participants are invited to share their reasons for positioning themselves in the space as they have done with the people closest to them. Finally, the organiser samples individual reasons for the choices made.

2 Various arguments about morality and justice are put forward in William Shakespeare's *Measure for Measure*. As a starting point for an exploration of the play two contrasting quotations were selected as follows.

> He who the sword of heaven will bear
> Should be as holy, as severe (Act 3, Scene 2)

> Why all the souls that were, were forfeit once,
> And he that might the vantage best have took
> Found out the remedy. How would you be
> If he, which is the top of judgement, should
> But judge you as you are? (Act 2, Scene 2)

Having discussed their understanding of the text, a **spectrum of difference** from True to False was set up for each quote to create the opportunity for group members to offer and debate individual choices in relation to the particular sentiments expressed.

Elaboration

This elaboration can be used with any spectrum-based convention. The idea is to fold over a spectrum from its mid-point so that individuals find themselves facing other group members who hold contrasting views. Participants can then pair up and discuss their contrasting positions and the reasons for the choices made.

More complex choices can also be addressed through a variation on **spectrum of difference**; the self-explanatory four corners.

 Taking sides

Description	As with the **spectrum of difference**, this convention requires group members to place themselves physically on an imaginary line (see Figure 7), this time linking two characters, indicating their preference through their choice of position. An open mind is indicated through placing oneself centrally, while the closer one stands to a chosen character, the stronger one's support. As a group's understanding of particular characters develops their support for and consequently their choices of position may well change.

> e.g. MOTHER ——————— Undecided ——————— CHILD

Figure 7 Spectrum of opinion (2)

Cultural connections	Voting; show of hands; taking a stand; Survey Monkey; online polls; Facebook polls; YouTube likes vs. dislikes.
Learning opportunities	Choosing and expressing personal analysis of human relationships; 'concretising' understandings in action; combining analysis with affective response.

Examples

1 Before playing with the story of The Three Little Pigs as told by the Wolf in Jon Scieszka's, *The True Story of the 3 Little Pigs* (Puffin, 1989), the group are asked to retell the story around the group with each participant telling as much of the traditional story as they feel comfortable to tell, before passing it on to the next person. Then each member of the group considers whether their sympathies lie currently with either wolf or pig and position themselves accordingly.

2 Johan August Strindberg's *Miss Julie* (Oxford World's Classics, 2008) explores the difficulties in relationships between people of different social class towards the end of the 19th century in Sweden.

The play tackles these challenging social issues through an exploration of the impossible and unequal relationship between Miss Julie, the headstrong daughter of an aristocrat, and Jean his manservant. At different points throughout the play the group are asked to place themselves on the **taking sides** spectrum on the basis of their preferences for either character.

This way/that way

Description	This is used as a means of pointing out the differences between various characters' interpretations of the same crucial event and thereby demonstrating that the points of view held may reflect the vested interests of the characters. The group act out each character's version of the event, paying attention to the detail of the differences and relating these details back to their understanding of the character.
Cultural connections	Witnesses for defence/prosecution in court cases; differences in newspaper accounts; party political broadcasts; tall stories; 'who started it in the first place?', and so on.
Learning opportunities	Allows group to detect and deconstruct the level of bias and prejudice in accounts given of the same event; encourages examination of the effect of class, race and gender interests on individual perspectives.

Examples

1 The group are using the following statement by Yellow Wolf of the Nez Percés, taken from Dee Brown's *Bury My Heart At Wounded Knee: An Indian History of the American West* (Vintage, 1987), as a starting point for looking at the colonisation of the American West: 'The whites told only one side. Told it to please themselves. Told much that is not true. Only his own best deeds, only the worst deeds of the Indians, has the white man told.'

2 As part of an investigative drama inquiring into the causes of a violent incident during a strike at a local factory, the group act out the event according to the conflicting accounts given in the press and in person by the national and local newspapers, the factory manager, a picket and the local police.

Thought shower

Description	Participants speak aloud the words and phrases that come into their minds while reflecting upon group experiences. Words, sentences and phrases can overlap the statements of others. Group members can repeat and emphasise their contributions as they see fit and both bounce off and pick up the contributions of others.
Cultural connections	Speaking your mind; finding a personal voice; collective responses at football matches, sports events, and so on; liking/disliking on websites.
Learning opportunities	Enables participants to quickly establish a personal response; makes the personal available to the group; combines analysis with affective response.

Examples

1   The group work on William Shakespeare's *Romeo and Juliet* Act 3, Scene 1, in which Tybalt kills Mercutio and Romeo takes his revenge. Romeo is sculpted at the moment he chooses to pick up a sword and attack Tybalt. The group have discussed Romeo's contrary emotions – he has just married Juliet, Tybalt is now his cousin – but Mercutio's death must be avenged.

The organiser speaks the line: 'O sweet Juliet / Thy beauty hath made me effeminate' – then group members rush Romeo, standing close about him to create the storm of thoughts and emotions running through his head. When this shower of thoughts reaches an intensity, the organiser claps, the shower stops and Romeo must decide what he does next.

2   Following a trip to interview seniors for a **reminiscence theatre** project, the group formed a standing circle with their arms about each other and **thought-showered** their initial thoughts, feelings and impressions about their visit as part of their group debrief.

Elaboration

The words and so on are collected and written on large sheets of paper and placed around the drama space to encourage further reflection.

Group members recite aloud those words and phrases that seem most meaningful to them. By a process of elimination they arrive at the key ideas for themselves and the group and through collective repetition create a social poem.

Thought-tracking

Description	This reveals publicly the private thoughts/reactions of participants-in-role at specific moments in the action so as to develop a reflective attitude towards the action and to contrast thinking-for-self with outward appearances or dialogue. Action may be frozen and participants 'tapped for thoughts', or thoughts may be prepared to go with the presentation of a **still-image**.
Cultural connections	Secrets; fears; hopes; keeping up appearances.
Learning opportunities	Devising thoughts requires reflection and analysis of situation and role; hearing other thoughts generates a sensitive/feeling response to the content; action is slowed down to allow for deeper understanding of meanings underlying action.

Examples

1   A group have reached the stage in exploring the traditional story of 'Hansel and Gretel' at which the children's father must decide whether or not to abandon his children in the forest. The group create a **still-image** of the father sitting forlornly considering his decision. Group members are able to go individually and stand with the father and then, placing a hand upon his shoulder, speak aloud the thoughts in his head at that particular moment in time.

2   As part of a sequence of work looking at 'Evacuees', half the group mime packing their bags with a parent in preparation for leaving; the other half speak out aloud what the participants might be thinking as they pack.

Elaboration

Often called Venting, this is a variation on **thought-tracking** in which participants can come up with and vent feelings, emotions, confusions and ambiguities in a character's mind at a particular moment in a drama. Several group members can vent simultaneously to create a 'dialogue' or to demonstrate different views of a character's state of mind.

Voices in the head

Description	The group use this as a means of reflecting on and deconstructing the complexity of a difficult choice. Others represent and speak aloud the discordant thoughts in the character's mind, or act as the conflicting elements of a collective conscience that evidences an interior dialogue and compares and contrasts advice based on moral or political choices. It is possible to develop this convention by allowing the character to interact directly with the voices and thus challenge the advice being offered; moreover, the voices themselves may engage in debate while the character listens in.
Cultural connections	Voice-over in film, television; chorus and strophe/antistrophe in Greek drama; use of asides in theatre.
Learning opportunities	Character becoming aware; others express, become involved in and influence the complexity of the imminent action; adds tension and slows action down to allow for reflection.

Examples

1 Working on Shakespeare's *Macbeth*, participants create the chaos and confusion in Macbeth's mind immediately following his meetings with the witches and with Lady Macbeth upon his return from battle. Macbeth's emotional turmoil is played out against a backdrop of **still-images** depicting events from the recent battle, moments of past loyalty and the possibilities of impending betrayal and future power.

2 During a drama around ideas from Graham Swift's *The Sweetshop Owner* (Picador, 2010), the following extract is explored first through discussion around **the iceberg** convention and then it is used as the focus for improvisation.

> Dear Father
>
> I have the £15,000. The bank notified me last week. Thank you for sending it at last. I'm sure this is for the best and how Mother would have wanted it. You will see in the end.
>
> I think we can call everything settled now. Don't bother about the rest of my things. You said I should come – do you really think that's a good idea? After all that you say I've put you through, I should have thought you'd be glad to finish with me at last.
>
> Dorothy

As an actor plays Dorothy, the remainder of the group provide the conflicting emotions in her mind as she writes the letter, speaking aloud each line of text as she writes.

Wall of China

Description	The group is asked to form a wall of 'protection' and 'defence' around a territory, idea, group or individual. One by one, members of the group make a physical wall.
	They can:
	face in and name what it is that they are protecting or what they worry might be tainted or even 'stolen' by outsiders
	or
	face out and name a threat, a menace or a fear about the 'outside' world, or the unknown which lies beyond
	or
	link hands with others and state what binds this territory, idea, or group together as a community or as a coalition.
Cultural connections	Football players protecting goal; castles, fortifications, barricades; inhibitions; self-protection strategies; geographical borders and nationhood; psychological barriers.
Learning opportunities	Participants have to reflect on what is to be protected and valued and what are the vulnerabilities and insecurities within the boundaries of the 'wall'. They must also reflect on the threats and fears about 'outsiders'. This may involve some discussion of who and what is included and excluded by the 'wall'.

Examples

1   In a drama about the experiences of refugees, the group create and name the physical borders and fences created to keep out illegal immigrants, what these fences are supposed to protect and what they are supposed to keep out – in other words how refugees and other immigrants are seen as a 'threat'. They also imagine the psychological 'wall' that a refugee might build around themselves in order to protect themselves and their culture when they find 'shelter' in a new country or culture.

2   As an extension of the above, the group use physical movement to show how the 'wall' reacts when there is a 'threat' – is it welcoming or aggressively protective? They consider what kind of 'unity' the 'wall' provides – how does it unite the people or ideas or groups on the inside of the 'wall'? How does it mark out the difference between outsiders and insiders? The group also considers how culture and beliefs can, like a 'wall', also unite and protect people who may be in different places. Using their bodies to show

thorough gesture and dance-like movement whether they are welcoming or aggressively protecting, they can react physically as another group playing 'outsiders' move nearer or further away from the 'Wall'.

3 The group is working on 'Dear Diary' extracts from David Grossman's teen novel *Someone to Run With* (Bloomsbury Publishing PLC, 2004) and have begun to create a central protagonist as the focus for their developing exploration, taking the quote: 'If the world doesn't understand me, the world is not the world.' They stand in a line in front of a **still-image** they have created of the protagonist and, facing outwards from the image, each participant names the teenage threat that the protagonist most fears about the 'adult' world.

Walls have ears

Description	The group make the four walls of a room by standing in lines around a previously crafted **still-image** of the protagonist. They then collectively reflect back impressions of the key events that have befallen that character through snatches and repetition of dialogue, sound, and so on.
Cultural connections	Folk-belief that the stones of a building absorb the emotional experiences of the people who live within.
Learning opportunities	Enables participants to synthesise the elements of a series of experiences based around the exploration and development of a character; to find form for their personal affective response.

Examples

1   A group exploring Jim Cartwright's play *Road* (Methuen Drama, 1990) have worked from the monologue delivered by a character called Val to create a detailed picture of her home life. Val lives with a profligate husband and frequently has to borrow from friends to feed her children. The group set up **walls have ears** at a point in the drama where Val sits alone staring at her husband's empty armchair and the participants mix echoes of happier times, such as Val's courtship, with the sadness of the eventual breakdown of her marriage.

2   At the midpoint of a drama centred on the family problems of a young woman, the group use **walls have ears** as a device to review and focus the growing intensity of family rows until the point at which the young woman reluctantly makes the decision to leave home. Then, with a clearer understanding of the pressures acting on the family, the group move on to explore possible futures.

Window on the world

Description	This convention allows a group to record and reflect upon information about a character and his or her ongoing relationships as the details are uncovered by the group through either rehearsal or devising. Four large sheets of paper are arranged as though they were the panes of glass in a window. Each of the four panes represents the different ways in which a central character is perceived:

- The first represents how the character sees his or her own self.
- The second shows how the character is seen by the people or person they are most intimate with.
- The next represents how a friend would see the character.
- The final sheet represents how an acquaintance or even a complete stranger would perceive the character.

The group write their observations and character analyses in the appropriate sections as their exploratory work discloses detail. Where necessary they also add a brief character sketch of the people whose viewpoints they record.

Cultural connections	Facebook friends; YouTube subscribers; Twitter followers; six degrees of separation; social networks and networking.
Learning opportunities	Allows the group the opportunity to focus and debate their growing understandings and perceptions of a character; offers opportunities to record and reflect upon a character's wider and more immediate circles; provides an ongoing record of the outcome of character interpretation and analysis.

Example

1 At the end of a first read-through of Anton Chekhov's *The Cherry Orchard* (*Chekhov Plays*, Penguin Books, 1977) the group are asked to return to the text for the necessary clues, and then to use the **window on the world** diagram as the focus for discussion and to record their initial observations of Mme Ranyevskaia and her relationships with particular characters. They list them as follows.

Self: Mme Liubov Andryeevna Ranyevskaia (Liuba). She holds on to her illusions. She is generous to a fault. She is in love with the idea of love. She is nostalgic for the past, for a time of security. 'I can't conceive life without the cherry orchard' (Act 3 p. 375). Although not capable of changing herself, or taking advice, she is still capable of introspection. She appreciates how foolish she has been: 'Oh, my sins! Look at the way I've squandered money, continually. It was sheer madness' (Act 2 p. 359). She can only see herself going on as before and at the play's end returns to Paris and her unsatisfactory life there.

Significant others: Gayev, her idle and effete brother. He is a baby, a spoilt brat who has never needed to grow up. The status quo in Russia is changing too fast for Gayev. A constant social catastrophe, he does at least try to dissuade Liuba from spending. However, his love for Liuba and his lack of drive mean that in the end he can achieve nothing.

Ania, her daughter, shares her mother's viewpoint entirely. She loves home and agonises over the fate of the orchard. Ania is sensitive and caring like her mother; she comforts her with: 'don't cry, Mamma, you still have your life ahead of you, you still have your dear, innocent heart' (Act 3 p. 385).

Friends: Lopakhin is a self-made businessman whose parents were peasants. He offers advice to Liuba, which is rejected, and so he buys the orchard himself. In Act 2, Lopakhin says of Liuba and Gayev: 'I've never met such feckless, unbusiness-like people as you are' (Act 2. p. 358). He has fond memories of Liuba from childhood, but these memories tie him to the past, so in order to break free, he must forget his gratitude to Liuba.

Trofimov is the eternal student and both judgmental and unforgiving. Trofimov was Liuba's dead son's tutor and brings bad memories with him. He has no real world experience and yet thinks he can lecture Liuba. He thinks he understands the changing world better than she does. He sees himself as the future and views Liuba as the past.

Acquaintances/Strangers: Pishchik, Liuba's neighbour. He sees her as a soft touch and a ready source of funds.

Feers an ancient manservant. Possibly senile, he has an automatic respect for Liuba. The family mean to get him to hospital, but it never happens and he lies alone and forgotten at the end of the play.

The Stranger/Tramp is a reminder of the real world beyond the bubble in which Liuba lives. Liuba offers him a gold coin. He must think she is a goddess. A being from another planet.

As their understandings of the characters and the text develop, they return to the diagram to add and make changes as necessary. At the same time, they also consider Liuba's gaze back through the window and her view of the other characters.

Part 2   Structuring drama for learning opportunities

Introduction

The conventions detailed in the previous section give some indication of the forms available for working through theatre. The purpose of this section is to identify possible **processes** that may enable participants and organisers to make creative use of the conventions in order to create opportunities for learning. The processes described in this section are based on a set of common assumptions about theatre as a learning medium, the purposes of a 'conventions approach' to learning through theatre and principles of practice that guide structuring drama for learning opportunities.

Assumptions about theatre processes and forms

Historically, theatre has always drawn its content from a broad sweep of human experience. Its conventions have evolved through the need to provide entertainment and illumination through the accurate, critical and sensuous depiction of individuals and groups engaged in the business of living in the world, within a variety of socio-historical contexts.

In common with other narrative forms, such as story and film, theatre frames and represents aspects of human experience and social concepts through the isolation and portrayal of specific examples that are representative of a broader area of human experience. The success of a theatrical activity is partly judged on its ability to subsume an important area of human experience within a particular set of fictional circumstances, situations and characters.

Theatre triggers similar psychological processes to other narrative art forms, such as novels, poetry and film. In other words, it harnesses the basic, natural and spontaneous human ability to make and respond to stories, told in words and pictures, which help a storyteller to symbolise her sense of the world and an audience to see and hear the world from another's perspective.

In order to make its stories, or 'representations of experience', the conventions of theatre utilise dimensions of form that are shared with conventions in other art forms as well as dimensions that are unique to theatre.

1 Language

In common with most other art forms, language is used in theatre as the organising medium for discussing, planning and implementing ideas; group work comes out of talk about the task; a director will use language to describe ideas to actors. Language is also used symbolically as a means of representing a situation or a character's speech (as it might also be used in the narrative forms of story, prose, poetry and film).

However, theatre does not wholly depend on the symbolic use of language in the same way narrative forms (other than film) do in order to describe places, relationships or action. A 1 **still-image**, for example, uses space, gesture and objects, rather than words, to represent places, relationships and action. Because theatre is a visual as well as an aural medium, meanings are often communicated through an interplay between what is seen and what is said.

2 Relationships of time

In common with other narrative forms, the way in which certain conventions interact with the experience of time is a central feature of theatre-form. In literary forms, narrative sometimes follows a natural sequence of time where one event follows another chronologically, but it can also use conventions that fracture and distort a natural sequence – flashbacks/flash-forwards; letters; third-person commentary, and so on. In theatre the same is true: time either unfolds at life-rate or is taken to be a completely elastic material that can be stopped, accelerated and replayed through the use of conventions.

The experience of time in theatre is distinguished by the fact that 'action' in other narrative forms (novels, poems, film) is usually reported and past for the reader, whereas action in theatre is always in the 'here and now' for the audience and actors (even if the action belongs to a historical event). Because theatre is a narrative form, the here-and-now experience of a dramatic moment is enhanced by the expectation that something else is about to happen; interest in the here-and-now is held by the promise of what begins to happen next. Theatre is live, but it is also transient and ephemeral; it only exists for as long as the performance lasts. It is not permanent in the way that film and other recorded narrative forms are.

3 Relationships of space

Certain conventions focus on the symbolic use of space in order to convey meanings either in terms of movements in space, as in dance, or in the way in which space is arranged and used to provide a visual context, or reinforcement for meanings associated with levels of status between characters, physical surroundings and psychological distance in relationships.

The relevance of space to meaning-making in theatre is evidenced in scripts where 'directions' are given to indicate to actors appropriate moves and gestures to accompany dialogue. The importance of space is also evidenced in the term 'Scene', which associates a section of action with a place or use of space. In performance there is often a division of space that defines an acting area; the expectation is that any movement or use of space in the defined area will be symbolic and meaningful for the spectators.

In improvisation work space may be used more intuitively, with an emphasis on discovering the possibilities of space as the drama unfolds, but awareness of how space is being used is still profoundly important to the meaning-making process and to helping participants build confidence in the drama. The question of how the available space might be used to give additional meaning to the action, or to build the participants' belief in the action, is as important as are questions to do with role and situation.

4 Social interaction

As in certain kinds of music activity and in dance, theatre is a social and collective form that depends on the creative interaction between the skills of actors/spectators/writers/technicians/designers/directors. Interaction occurs in two dimensions:

a The *real dimension* of discussion, planning, organising and reviewing
b The *symbolic dimension* when participants are interacting and behaving symbolically within a convention that temporarily supersedes the real dimension.

Immediately before going on stage actors may interact in the real dimension, but once on stage they can only communicate through the words and actions of their characters. Actors faced with a problem in the real dimension while on stage (such as might be caused by the non-appearance of a vital prop or another character skipping a scene) will struggle to manage the real problem by improvising with each other in character within the symbolic dimension.

This experience of managing the real dimension from within the symbolic dimension is central to the learning experience of improvisational forms of drama. The challenge and thrill for groups in conventions such as **teacher-in-role**, **meetings**, **hot-seating** and **voices in the head** is that they have to manage signals and communications in the real dimension from within the convention. Real anxieties or questions have to find expression through the symbolic dimension if the convention is to be sustained. For example, an individual may be confused by the identity of a character who is being **hot-seated**. Rather than breaking the convention, a question has to be asked, in context, to reveal the character's identity without forcing the character to break role and respond in the real dimension. This subtle interchange between the real and symbolic, which is necessary to the successful management of improvisational conventions, makes substantial demands on groups, but also provides substantial rewards.

In the symbolic dimension channels of communication and the participants' behaviour are deliberately limited by the nature of the conventions that are being used to create meaning. In **small-group play-making**, for instance, the actors are confined to speech and behaviour that belong to the characters and action they are representing, and the spectators are confined to waiting until the actors have finished before commenting. In **forum-theatre**, on the other hand, the convention allows the spectators to interrupt and comment on the action as it unfolds, and the actors agree to be influenced by the spectators' suggestions and modelling.

Assumptions about purpose

The learning potential of theatre, as an arts-process, lies in the participants' conscious and critical realisation of the relationships created between the content-area of a drama (some aspect of human experience) and the conventions used to engage with that content. Therefore, knowledge of the conventions is useful only in so far as it enables meaningful content to be productively 'handled', demonstrated and experienced by those taking part in the dramatic activity. Within this view, the conventions of theatre are seen as vehicles for experiencing and communicating meanings symbolically. Using the matching of convention to content in order to depict and transform personal and social meanings is the process of theatre.

Knowledge and understanding of the ways in which conventions and content interact in theatre allow participants to develop a critical consciousness of the work of playwrights and the ideological bias within different styles and genres of theatre.

An imaginative and tuned awareness of the possibilities of the conventions and the demands made by them allows participants to isolate and simulate aspects of human experience for themselves.

Increasingly, abstract and complex concepts can be made concrete, communicable and open to examination through the participant's discovery and experience of different matches of convention and content. *The effect of the experience of translating ideas and concepts into 'here-and-now' symbolic action is to transform pre-existing thinking about the content.*

Principles for structuring theatre for learning opportunities

The brief set of principles below are used to guide the presentation of the approach to structuring suggested in this section as they might also be able to guide choices in the development of an improvised drama activity. They are based on the assumption that structures must alter and change according to circumstances rather than remain as rigid templates that ignore the here-and-now potential of theatre experience. Even in the performance of a 'fixed' text, the structure will be influenced by the experience of the actors, the responses of the audience, the venue and unforeseen circumstances. In improvised forms of drama, choices about how the drama might develop are a constant feature and it is useful to have a consistent set of principles to assist in making the appropriate choice of direction or action.

- Structuring should observe the agreed rights and dignity of those taking part and those who are represented in the work in both real and symbolic dimensions; at the very least this means matching conventions and content so as to remove, disturb and inhibit prejudicial and disempowering images of class, race, sexuality and gender.
- Choices about which conventions are used and which content is explored should respect the organiser's need to ensure that the work is controlled, purposeful and effective. (Different conventions pose different kinds of risk and demand for both participants and organiser.)
- Systematic opportunities should be provided for participants to make informed choices about conventions, content, structure and the meanings suggested by the work.
- Structuring should take into account the need to introduce conventions within the context of content relevant to, and representative of, the group's needs and current preoccupations.
- Structuring should combine personal and social learning arising from the content with aesthetic learning about the conventions of theatre.
- Participants should grow to see theatre as a powerful vehicle for challenging and changing attitudes towards the world and for the expression of a world-view.

- The dramatic activity should be punctuated by systematic and structured opportunities for personal, small-group and whole-group reflection that focuses on the personal and social demands made by the work in terms of:

  - exploring the moral, political, social and historical meanings emerging from the dramatic exploration of the content-area
  - understanding the changing effect the use of different conventions is having on the content (or on the group's original responses to the content)
  - analysing the interrelationships between convention and content
  - checking out any assumptions or values held by the group, or individuals working within the group, that are biasing or prejudicing the development of the work
  - checking out and balancing, if necessary, the emotional and skill demands made by the convention in use.

A process model for theatre in educational contexts

1 Starting point – identifying the content

The source material for dramatic activity of any kind will be rooted in human experience. To the individuals involved in the activity, the experience itself may be real, imagined, reported or historical. The source material may be:

a concept, such as 'freedom'	a story
a newspaper account	a photograph or painting
a playscript	a primary or secondary historical source
an image or sculpture	
a map or diagram	a poem
music and sounds	an object associated with the experience
	lyrics

The source is selected according to its ability to bring the experience into the intellectual and emotional comprehension of the participants (helping the group to make human contact with the experience), so that responses and questions can be shared and some element of the experience can be located within their own personal and collective experience. Some experiences, or human concepts, may be so far removed or so abstract that a source is required that makes the experience manageable for participants. For example the Mahabharata may serve as a source for an exploration of concepts of justice and fairness, as might the biblical story of Solomon. William Shakespeare's *Measure for Measure* may serve as a source for exploring the power of the State and the responsibilities of leadership, as might the Buddhist legend 'The Banyan Deer'. (Thus the examples given for the conventions described in Part 1 are intended to serve as 'sources' for making the experience of the convention understandable and manageable for readers.

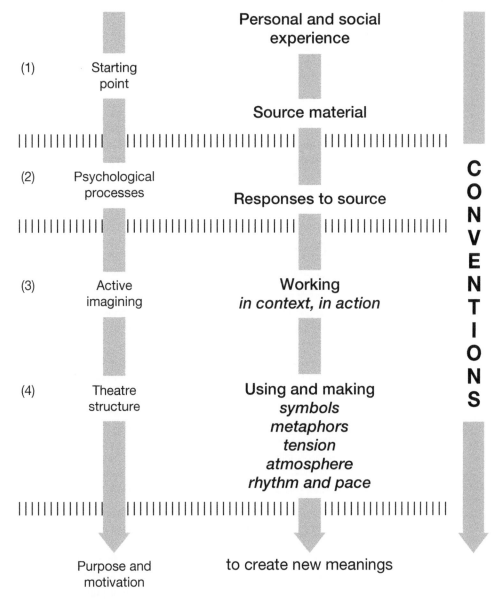

Personal and social experience

(1) Starting point

Source material

(2) Psychological processes

Responses to source

(3) Active imagining

Working *in context, in action*

(4) Theatre structure

Using and making *symbols metaphors tension atmosphere rhythm and pace*

Purpose and motivation

to create new meanings

CONVENTIONS

Figure 8   A process model for theatre in educational contexts

For the dramatic activity to be worthwhile, the source needs to find a response in those taking part; the experience of street theatre demonstrates that if an idea fails to interest and catch hold, nobody takes part or watches. The selection and introduction of a particular source as an appropriate starting point for dramatic activity is clearly a crucial matter; in context the selection of source may be influenced by its potential to:

- translate a human experience accurately into terms that can be recognised and understood by the participants
- represent the experience in an accessible combination of words, images and feelings
- immediately capture the interest and imagination of a group
- give sufficient information about an experience and engage feelings
- speak directly to the group's current preoccupations
- motivate a desire to seek further information
- trigger the natural need to make sense of clues given in the source through the construction of stories that flesh out the clues
- create an appropriate background of concerns and feelings amongst the group.

2 Psychological processes – establishing ownership

Part of the process of making a response to the source involves making imaginative and quizzical connections to the words, images and feelings that the source uses in order to represent the experience to which it relates. Participants may relate to all three, or they may find that individually it is easier to relate to representations in words, or in pictures, or in feelings. Because theatre is a collective and social activity, groups can pool their individual responses and work from an enhanced group response to the source. Because theatre uses words, images and feelings in its conventions, it is possible, in dramatic activity, to structure opportunities for responding by using conventions that release all three in a variety of combinations; this holds for devising, interpreting script and improvised drama.

In structuring for improvised drama, the organiser has the advantage of being able to introduce conventions as the activity develops to match or challenge the form of a particular group's response at different points in the drama. If the group's response is in images, then the organiser can choose to work in visual conventions, such as **still-image** or **mimed activity**. Alternatively, the organiser may wish to extend the response by introducing conventions that emphasise verbal communications, such as **role-reversal**, **teacher-in-role** or **telephone/radio conversations**.

3 Active imagining – from response to action

The nature of the conventions of theatre allows the participants to start using them fairly immediately in order to begin to bring the chosen experience, and their responses to it, into their own immediate 'here-and-now' experience. Agreement about an area of enquiry, a response or a particular place and moment suggested by the source (together with an agreement about the form and roles required by the convention that is to be used) allows participants to move into the symbolic dimension of theatre as a means of further developing their understanding both of the experience and of the convention. *It is an essential feature of theatre, as an educational medium, that it provides a means of bringing an experience into action and into context; it bypasses discussion and gives the signal for the participant's talk and activity to change to talk and activity that they imagine is representative of the experience itself.*

Certain conventions allow for a more immediate entry into theatre than others. For instance, the source might suggest to the participants possible responses to four basic questions:

- What questions do we want to ask?
- Whom do we want to question?
- Who might have an interest in asking the questions?
- Where and when would the questions be put?

These responses might lead in turn to the immediate use of:

Teacher-in-role	**Meetings**
Mantle of the expert	**Giving witness**
Interviews/interrogations	**Forum-theatre**
Hot-seating	**Voices in the head**

Alternatively, the source may suggest conventions that require group talk and activity geared towards a group presentation that fixes responses to the experience through:

Still-image	**Role-on-the-wall**
Simulations	**Re-enactment**
Diaries, letters, journals, messages	**Circle of life**
A day in the life	**Objects of character**
Small-group play-making	

Even where the entry into theatre is dependent on preliminary talk and activity, the group is immediately helped to make sense of the experience represented by the source through the preparatory work for the convention, which is context-building action, task-focused and intended to guide the group towards making the experience concrete, particular and manageable.

4 Theatre structure – generating meanings

Conventions define the form of the dramatic activity and how participants behave at particular stages of its development. *Structure describes the dynamic relationship that emerges between the stages of the drama – the relationship between conventions as the drama progresses.* The structural elements described here do not necessarily reside in separate conventions; rather they grow out of the progressive matching of conventions and content, which in turn leads to a development of understanding and experience.

Symbols It is in the nature of theatre that it is understood that objects, action and use of space have the capacity to become a focus for meanings that go beyond the literal. A chair may be understood to represent a throne – which in turn may develop into a focus for the representation of the relationship between the ruler and the ruled. The chair may be re-used in a variety of conventions so that it accumulates importance as a symbol for the focus of the work. The importance of symbols lies in their capacity to go on generating further and deeper meanings as the drama develops and also in their capacity to serve as *reference points* or *motifs* that bind the various stages of the development of the drama.

While all conventions (particularly poetic action conventions) have the potential to generate symbols, certain conventions tend to emphasise or produce symbols:

Ritual	**Ceremony**
Still-image	**Defining space**
Masks	**Re-enactment**
Diaries, letters, journals, messages	**Mimed activity**

Atmosphere In common with other art forms the atmosphere associated with a piece of dramatic activity is an important factor in generating responses. The construction of an appropriate atmosphere builds credibility and arouses feelings and moods that are both appropriate to the context and also experienced in a real way by both participants/actors and spectators/audience. Because theatre is always live, atmosphere has a special importance for the audience in creating levels of mood, context and circumstance.

In performance, atmosphere is generated for an audience through the tone and register of the actor's voice, the action, set and costume design, lighting, music and other effects. In improvised forms the same sources can be used to generate an appropriate atmosphere for the participants.

Certain conventions tend to emphasise and produce atmosphere:

Soundtracking	Masks
Thought-tracking in still-image	Prepared roles
Re-enactment	Teacher-in-role
Giving witness	Hot-seating
Ritual	Marking the moment

Tension Tension in theatre describes the different sources of mental or emotional arousal participants or an audience might experience during dramatic activity.

As in other narrative forms, narrative-action tensions may be invitations, or lures, to become committed and involved in the unfolding story or action. Examples of tension are:

- what will happen next
- a mystery
- a race against time
- becoming dependent on a person or natural resource
- a secret known to some but not to others
- an obstacle to be overcome in order for a situation to be resolved
- enduring a test or challenge
- a moral dilemma.

Tension in poetic-action conventions may also emerge in ways that are familiar in art forms such as music, dance and the visual arts through:

- counterpointing the use of space, sounds, movements
- contrasting:

  stillness/movement
  light/darkness
  sound/silence

- symbols that have ambiguous or contradictory meanings.

Social metaphor Symbolic action in theatre is understood to be representative of actions associated with actual experience. The purpose of metaphor in theatre, as in other art forms, is to invite comparison between what is being symbolically represented and the real area of experience that is referred to. Part of the learning experience of theatre is in recognising and constructing connections between the fiction of the drama and the real events and experiences the fiction draws on. *As the theatrical activity unfolds, the fictional situation and characters become more and* *more recognisable to the creators of the drama, and relationships begin to form between what is happening in the drama and what happens in the outside world.*

Rhythm and pace As in all other art forms, the conventions of theatre give participants the opportunity to suspend reality through representative uses of time, space and behaviour. Theatre provides the opportunity to rearrange the otherwise unalterable rhythm and pace of reality. Theatre concepts such as 'timing' and 'pacing' are as important to the experience of the drama as 'pulse' and 'rhythm' are in music. Audiences talk about performances being 'slow' and actors having 'good timing'. There are other important considerations when structuring drama for learning opportunities, for example, the need to establish a rhythm and pace that:

- allows for reflection
- moves at the right pace for all the participants to feel comfortable
- provides a variety of activity, group size and conventions
- balances active/still involvement and actor/spectator roles
- accommodates institutional constraints on time, space and noise levels.

Part 3   Theatre as a learning process

Within the presentation of theatre-process in Figure 1 there is an implicit suggestion of a mirror educational process that is based on the assumption that it should be geared to participants experimenting with theatre in an *active inquiry mode*, in order to discover more about human experience and the aesthetic possibilities of theatre through:

- the active study and performance of theatre texts
- experiencing, as spectators and as actors, a variety of world theatre styles and genres, as well as experiencing the diversity of conventions within each style
- using conventions to experience and to translate, depict and transform personal and social meanings.

An active inquiry using theatre involves participants engaging with complex areas of human experience in order to discover the questions and issues that are relevant to their needs and level of experience. The process of inquiry is cyclical and ongoing because the nature of theatre is to discover and rediscover new depths in the material in focus. An actor may have played Ophelia several times, but work on a new production offers the actor the opportunity to discover new facets and ambiguities in the role. A group may often have worked in drama on the theme of families, but a different starting point, or a fresh match of convention to theme, offers the possibility of new areas of inquiry and understanding. Because theatre is essentially concerned with the sweep of human experience, it tends to prompt new levels of questioning rather than to promote answers.

Theatre in an active-inquiry process

Figure 9 seeks to identify this educational process as a cyclical model based on certain key stages in the development of an active inquiry through theatre.

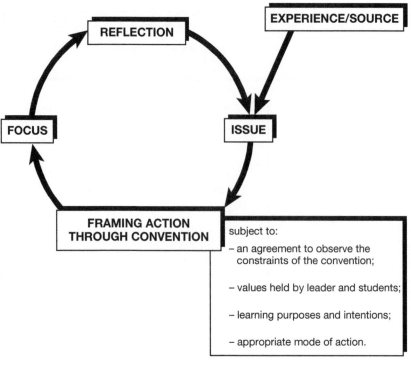

Figure 9   Theatre in an active-inquiry process

1 Experience/source → issue

(See also Part 2, A process model for theatre in educational contexts, 1. Starting point – identifying the content.)

Discussion and responses to the source will move towards the identification of those content-focused issues that will form the basis for the inquiry through theatre. The issues may relate to:

(a) *Problems of meaning – how to find depth in the source*
- questions about the logic and sequence of events described
- speculations about the wider context of the source
- personal and social issues triggered by the source
- questions about motivation, intentions, consequences of actions referred to in the source
- curiosities about the people and events described.

(b) *Problems of form – how to translate the experience into theatre*
- how to stage or how to re-enact events described in the source
- how to set up a situation for improvisation that will relate to the experience described
- how to apply techniques, skills and conventions in order to open up the material
- how to find and exploit the dramatic potential in the material in order to realise and convey symbols, atmosphere, metaphor and tension.

2 Framing action through convention

(See also Part 2, A process model for theatre in educational contexts, 3. Active imagining – from response to action.)

This stage in the process is reached when there is sufficient commitment to the idea of exploring the area of experience identified through the source and the group's responses to the source.

The transition from discussion about the issues involved to behaving and talking 'in context, in action' is a delicate shift into theatre. The success of this transition is likely to be determined by an agreement amongst the majority, if not all, of those present to *observe the constraints* of the conventions on role behaviour and the imagined uses of time, space and presence.

Making an effective match depends on a careful consideration of a variety of factors relating to the personal, social and aesthetic needs of the group and the organiser, as well as to the issue arising from the content. In choosing a convention, the organiser will seek an appropriate match with the issues identified, but the choice will be limited by:

- the values the organiser seeks to promote or exclude
- the value the participants place on the process as a form of inquiry and their willingness to participate as actors and/or spectators
- the learning intentions underlying the inquiry
- the mode of action that is appropriate to the personal/social needs in the group and the aesthetic development of the inquiry.

Observing the constraints – agreeing to suspend disbelief

For dramatic activity of any kind to take place, participants need to agree to behave in ways that make it possible for theatre to happen. The dominant performance tradition in Western lyric theatre, for example, requires an audience who agree to remain silent, fixed and virtually invisible for the duration of the performance, and in return actors agree to confine their behaviour and speech to that which is consistent with the imagined experience they are representing for the audience. The audience agree to discuss and comment after the actors have signalled the end of their work. Each of the conventions described in this book requires participants to agree to constrain their behaviour in specific ways, and to adopt roles that reflect the roles of spectator and actor.

The nature of the agreement required will vary from one convention to another; some conventions will require subtle/complex agreements:

- In **hot-seating**, for instance, an agreement is made that one or more of the group will speak and behave as if they were characters involved in the drama. The rest of the group agree either to behave as spectators by allowing the characters to speak or to ask the characters appropriate questions without challenging the illusion. The agreement may also include the idea that other participants can only ask questions that are appropriate to a particular role, such as scientists, detectives, newspaper reporters, and so on.
- In whole-group dramas supported by **teacher-in-role**, participants agree to fuse the roles of actor and spectator so that a participant restricts herself to talk and behaviour appropriate to someone who is part of the fictional experience – even if, psychologically, she is more of a detached spectator watching and following the fictional behaviour of others who are more involved as actors. An agreement is often made to hold questions and comments belonging to the real dimension until the symbolic dimension offered by the role-play is suspended.

The agreement required by a theatre convention is more easily secured if those taking on the roles of spectators and actors have elected to be present through choice and have an inquisitive interest both in the content and in the form of the performance or dramatic experience. In educational contexts, however, this is often not the case. Within any group there may be a range of commitment – from those committed to the drama, through those who are uncomfortable with the idea, to those who are only there because they are forced to be so. The decision to proceed into dramatic action in certain educational contexts is, therefore, a difficult one to make. The decision might be influenced by evidence that:

- the source has aroused sufficient enthusiasm to consider suggesting theatre as a way forward
- a workable proportion of the group feel ready to observe the convention that is suggested as an introduction to the dramatic work
- moving into theatre is likely to increase rather than diminish a possibly low level of initial commitment to the project
- an appropriate match of content and convention can be made
- preliminary discussion has allowed participants to make choices between conventions suggested as starting points for the action and also to make choices about whether they wish to participate as spectators or actors
- participants are clear about the intentions of the work in terms of how it might develop understanding of both convention and chosen content.

Organiser values on content An active-inquiry mode of working suggests an openness to the idea that participants should discover and make their own meanings out of the content as a result of their work in drama. In practice, the range of available meanings is likely to be constrained by organiser concern to filter choices about the match of convention to content in order to promote certain values through the work and also to resist the emergence of other values. There is, of course, a tradition in theatre of the voices of the playwright and director dominating the work of actors and others involved in the performance and, as a result, also dominating the range of meanings communicated to the audience. The same is inevitably true for the organiser involved in the process of matching convention to content.

Improvised drama tends to allow participants a greater freedom to be actively involved in the matching process, but even so the organiser may wish to avoid a match of convention to content that might produce responses that will ultimately deny the dignity of, or exclude, individuals in the group or the people they represent in the drama on the basis of gender, social class, ability, sexuality, ethnicity or age. In preventing the portrayal of deficit images, the organiser is also positively promoting values such as tolerance, fairness, justice, compassion and respect for others. The force of organiser involvement (or lack of it) will be influenced by his/her own moral and political ideologies.

The choice of convention may also be limited in instances where the organiser gauges that the material is becoming uncomfortable and over-threatening for individuals in the group, and that the use of certain conventions may increase the problem.

In very general terms, **narrative-action** conventions, because they emphasise events and work at a relatively fast pace, may encourage superficial or poorly considered responses, whereas well-researched **context-building action** and the controlled pace of **reflective action** may produce challenges to assumptions and prejudices.

The process of matching convention content to the needs of the group is underpinned by the assumption that the organiser is working with a consistent and explicit set of **principles** that check and guide intervention in the participants' choice of convention, and also that the organiser is planning to ensure that an improvisation allows for fresh insights to be developed within a framework of constraints.

Teacher-in-role (TiR) is a particularly sensitive way for the organiser to initiate changes in the direction of the drama, challenges to thinking, shifts in action and new conventions from within the symbolic dimension, i.e. to manage the real needs and concerns of the group from within the drama. In an active-inquiry mode of working it is particularly important to make reference to reflective/ evaluative questions that clearly indicate the level of advantage the organiser is taking in the drama through **TiR**, and to ensure that responses to the questions are consistent with the principles.

The following questions are designed to assist those who wish to use the **TiR** convention as a central resource for initiating, developing and managing a drama.

- **What information is being given?**
  - about the context
  - about the situation
  - about the roles the group are being invited to adopt.

- **What atmosphere is the role generating?**
  - through selection of: vocabulary; register (linguistic); tone; category of action; volume; costume/props; spatial relationships.

- **What doors are being opened to the group?**
  - clues as to what needs doing by whom
  - a definition of the problem
  - possibilities for interaction
  - what human themes and issues are being introduced
  - indications as to what sort of 'destinations' the group might travel to in the drama.

- **What doors are kept closed?**
  - parameters of the action defined by role
  - decisions made by the organiser rather than by the group in response to the role
  - clues as to who will hold the balance of power in the interaction.

- **Where is the challenge?**
  - Is a task being set?
  - Is the role going to cause a disturbance within an existing situation?
  - Is a request for help being made?
  - What demands are going to be made on the group?

- **What tension is being created by the role's presence?**
  - What affective tension will hold the 'game' of the drama together and provide a motive for joining in? Possible tensions might include:

    tension of secrecy
    tension of mystery
    tension of an obstacle to overcome

tension of time
tension of dare/personal challenge/test
tension of dependence on another
tension of status to be challenged.

- **What controls are within the role's behaviour?**
  - Are implicit/explicit 'rules' introduced by the role?
  - How is the group's attention held?
  - What attempts are made to focus the group's activity or verbal responses?
  - Where is the source of the role's authority:

    in its status
    in its situation
    in its spectacle.

Group values on theatre as a learning process The match of convention to content also depends on the value the group place on dramatic activity as a useful and meaningful means of handling the source material. Because theatre uses the whole person for expression, there is a considerable risk for participants who cannot, without feeling threatened, let go of their concerns and pressures in the *real* dimension in order to move into the exposure of the *symbolic* dimension. Equally, individuals may be conditioned to expect theatre to be a low-level learning activity to which they find it difficult to give commitment. *Matching requires negotiation over the level of risk and commitment a group are prepared to make.*

The conventions allow for considerable flexibility over levels and degrees of involvement. Certain conventions often assume whole-group participation by limiting responses to the symbolic dimension of the drama (by only allowing responses-in-role):

Teacher-in-role	**Meetings**
Still-image	**Mantle of the expert**

Other conventions allow for a small group of 'actors-by-choice' and a larger group of 'spectators-by-choice' to be involved in the direction and improvisation of the drama; they also allow for the roles of spectator and actor to be picked up, exchanged and dropped when participants choose to do so:

Forum-theatre	**Hot-seating**
A day in the life	**Voices in the head**
Narration	**Moment of truth**
Giving witness	**Tag-role**

Within each convention there are further variables. For example, **hot-seating** often suggests the idea of there being one or more actors sitting in a chair, responding to questions from a group of spectators who may or may not be in roles themselves. There may be a reason why a group does not produce any volunteers for **hot-seating**. If so, there are a number of variables that may assist the group's use of the convention:

- The organiser can take the role and be questioned by the group as themselves.
- An empty chair can symbolise the role and the group can collectively respond, in the role's words, to questions asked.
- The organiser can put the questions to the empty chair and then ask the group to respond with what they think the role's thinking might be, or what their own response might be.

Experimenting with the use of conventions and the roles of actor and spectator allows the group to control a subtle and gradual shift from the real to the symbolic. For example, action can grow from the group using furniture and other objects to represent the place where they imagine the drama is taking place and from them talking about the space, its atmosphere and what is in it. Figures can be placed in the space to represent where characters might be at a particular moment in the drama – conversation about placing the figures will start the process of theatre-action for the group. The group can suggest motives, thoughts and words for the figures, as themselves or symbolically through conventions such as **voices in the head** or **thought-tracking**. As interest grows in the context, the group may feel ready to enter the scene and interact together. But even if they do not, they have already begun to engage with theatre while appearing only to be commenting on the way in which they have visualised the scene of the drama.

Intentions for the work A further consideration in the matching process is the short- and long-term intentions of the work: the purposes underlying the group's use of theatre. The historic functions of theatre as an educative medium demonstrate that it is used in a variety of contexts that, briefly summarised, stretch from the psychotherapeutic through documentary, satiric and didactic to cathartic entertainment. In educational contexts there is evidence that theatre is used for a wide range of purposes – often as part of a structured developmental programme that organises learning purposes in the form of a syllabus to be followed, or as programmes of study leading to specific attainment targets. In common with other art forms, both the long- and short-term educational objectives for theatre work can be classified within a compass-type model that has four points of reference (as shown in Figure 10):

- **Instrumental objectives**
  Specific, measurable goals relating to skill development, conceptual development and knowledge.

- **Expressive objectives**
  Unspecific, indeterminate goals relating to the participant's development of attitudes and values, which may or may not occur through involvement in the dramatic action.

- **Aesthetic learning**
  Skills, concepts and knowledge relating to the art form.

- **Personal and social learning**
  Skills, concepts and knowledge relating to self and the 'self/ others' areas of learning provided in both the symbolic and real dimensions of the drama.

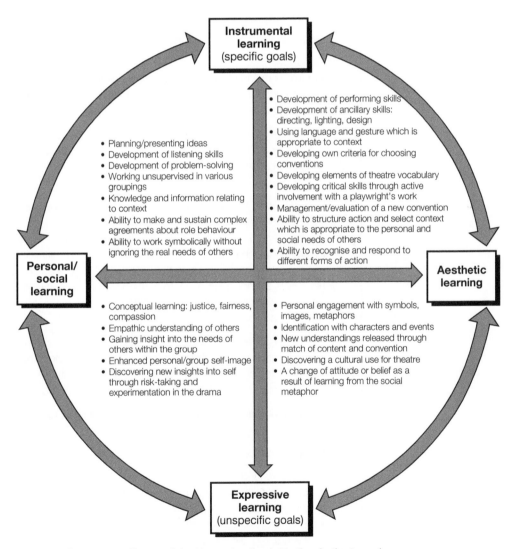

Instrumental learning (specific goals)

- Development of performing skills
- Development of ancillary skills: directing, lighting, design
- Using language and gesture which is appropriate to context
- Developing own criteria for choosing conventions
- Developing elements of theatre vocabulary
- Developing critical skills through active involvement with a playwright's work
- Management/evaluation of a new convention
- Ability to structure action and select context which is appropriate to the personal and social needs of others
- Ability to recognise and respond to different forms of action

- Planning/presenting ideas
- Development of listening skills
- Development of problem-solving
- Working unsupervised in various groupings
- Knowledge and information relating to context
- Ability to make and sustain complex agreements about role behaviour
- Ability to work symbolically without ignoring the real needs of others

Personal/ social learning

Aesthetic learning

- Conceptual learning: justice, fairness, compassion
- Empathic understanding of others
- Gaining insight into the needs of others within the group
- Enhanced personal/group self-image
- Discovering new insights into self through risk-taking and experimentation in the drama

- Personal engagement with symbols, images, metaphors
- Identification with characters and events
- New understandings released through match of content and convention
- Discovering a cultural use for theatre
- A change of attitude or belief as a result of learning from the social metaphor

Expressive learning (unspecific goals)

Figure 10 Classification of long- and short-term educational objectives for theatre work

Categories of action It is important to consider the category of action best suited to the issue that is to become the focus of the drama:

Context-building

Does the space need rearranging to represent the context for the action physically? Do characters need creating or fleshing out? Is any additional contextual information necessary?

Narrative

Is there a need to clarify the story or to move it on through action? Will narrative action breed commitment to the drama through the strength of the storyline?

Poetic

Do the group need to concentrate on making and communicating the symbols and images that represent their responses to the drama?

Reflective

Are things moving too quickly? Is there a need for action that requires consideration and thought? Is there a need for clarifying responses through the action?

Within each category, a further set of choices is available according to whether a direct or indirect form of entry is appropriate and what balance of spectators/actors is required either by the content or by the group.

Understanding the demands and functions of the conventions described in Part 1 gives the group and the organiser the opportunity to make a match of convention to content that reflects the factors outlined above. The conventions offer a multiplicity of routes into the material. As an illustration, the list of ideas presented here gives an indication of some of the possibilities of matching convention to content for a group using theatre as a way of exploring a short story.

The challenge, and the satisfaction, for the organiser lies in the level of creativity required to establish a priority order for the factors that will determine the appropriate match of convention to content for a group at a particular stage of its personal, social and aesthetic development.

Conventions as a means of deepening responses to a short story

Narrative action

Story conventions
- story told from different points of view
- incidents talked about between pairs of characters
- people outside the story commenting on the characters and events, e.g. teachers, neighbours, social workers, relatives
- scenes representing the group's prediction of the next part

- telephone conversations in which one character tells another what has been happening.

Role-play conventions
- **hot-seating** characters about their motives and reactions
- alternative scenes involving the characters
- **forum-theatre** looking at alternative courses of action to those described in the story
- outline of character put up on wall and 'role' built during the reading of the story
- organiser in the role of one of the characters as a starting point, or interviewed by the group
- meetings of characters, e.g. the villagers, parish council, chaired by the organiser or member of the group
- 'outside' broadcasts, news stories, chat shows involving characters or events from the story.

Context-building action

Still-image conventions
- tableaux representing 'illustrations' to key events
- family, or group, photographs – possibly contrasting public formal photos with private intimate photos
- tableaux representing events in the past or future
- freeze-frame convention as a way of holding action.

Physical-context conventions
- letters, diaries or notes written by, or between, characters
- precious or important objects drawn or made by the group
- designing or drawing costumes
- working space rearranged to represent an important 'space', e.g. a room, a cabin, or some other environment
- compiling oral reports, dossiers, records, secret files.

3 Focus – learning through discovery and imagined experience

(See also Part 2, A process model for theatre in educational contexts, 4. Theatre structure – generating meanings.)

As the work progresses, the participant's awareness of the content-area will develop and change as a result of her responses to the 'here-and-now' experience provided through the action of the convention. Contextual atmosphere is created, symbols and images emerge, the participant speaks and walks as another person and works with friends who are also projecting fictional roles. *It happens in all forms of theatre that the live experience of acting and spectating in itself begins the transformation of understandings about the area of experience that is represented in the drama.* It has already been suggested in this book that one of the unique qualities of theatre, as an arts medium, is that it is live, shared and subjectively experienced through its special uses and variations of time, space and human presence. Until the work starts, an artist – in any medium – is unlikely to have a clear idea of what a new piece of work should communicate or represent. She wants to discover her intentions through pitching her own individuality together with the ambiguities, dilemmas and mysteries suggested by an outline idea or expression through the craft of her art form or chosen material.

If groups involved in theatre are to gain practical experience as artists, rather than spend their time as participants learning about artists, then the organiser needs to allow focus to emerge through the work and through the choices that the participants make about the course of their work. *To be too definite and clear about the intentions and focus of the work in advance is to deny participants the power and experience of being artists.*

Certain formal, institutionalised contexts make it difficult for organisers, to work in this way. Institutional contexts that promote a climate of accountability based on the delivery of measurable, predetermined set tasks in pursuit of set goals press the organiser using theatre towards expressing only the instrumental features of their work at the expense of the vital, but indeterminate, expressive features.

4 Reflection – time out

(See also Part 2, Principles for Structuring Theatre for Learning Opportunities.)

As artists progress, they tend to take time away from their work in order to consider its development and what is being discovered as a result of working on the material. This reflection involves skills of perception, forming hypotheses, considering the tools and methods available and deciding on the next action before moving back to the work. *The reflective activity of the artist is likely to focus on the duality of the convention-to-content relationship; in other words, ideas about the content grow alongside ideas about how the medium or chosen material can be used to shape and communicate meanings.*

Acknowledgements

The authors and publishers acknowledge the following sources of copyright material and are grateful for the permissions granted. While every effort has been made, it has not always been possible to identify the sources of all the material used, or to trace all copyright holders. If any omissions are brought to our notice, we will be happy to include the appropriate acknowledgements on reprinting.

p. 31 excerpt from *Sula* by Toni Morrison, copyright © 1973 by Toni Morrison. Used by permission of Alfred A Knopf, an imprint of the Knopf Doubleday Publishing Group, a division of Penguin Random House LLC. All rights reserved. Any third party use of this material, outside of this publication, is prohibited. Interested parties must apply directly to Penguin Random House LLC for permission. Also published by Chatto & Windus, reprinted by permission of The Random House Group Limited;

p. 38 from *Junk* by Melvin Burgess, published and used by permission of Andersen Press;

p. 39 from *The Telling of Lies* by Timothy Findley, published and used with permission of Macmillan, copyright © Timothey Findley, 1992

p. 42 from *I'll Take You to Mrs Cole* by Nigel Gray (illustrated by Michael Foreman), Andersen Press, text © 1985 by Nigel Gray;

p. 57 excerpt from *The Handmaid's Tale* by Margaret Atwood. Copyright © 1985, 1986 by O.W. Toad, Ltd. Reprinted by permission of Houghton Mifflin Harcourt Publishing Company, McClelland & Stewart, a division of Penguin Random House Canada Limited, a Penguin Random House Company, and The Random House Group Limited. All rights reserved;

p. 63 excerpt from *The Caretaker and the Dumb Waiter*, copyright © 1960, 1988 by Harold Pinter. Used by permission of Grove/Atlantic, Inc. Any third party use of this material, outside of this publication, is prohibited;

p. 71 excerpt from *Witches Abroad* by Terry Pratchett, first published by Victor Gollancz, 1991, used by permission of The Orion Publishing Group London;

p. 78 excerpt from *The Wig My Father Wore* copyright © 1995 by Anne Enright. Used by permission of Grove/Atlantic, Inc. Any third party use of this material, outside of this publication, is prohibited. Also published by The Random House Group Limited;

p. 89 lines from 'There is no sorrow' from *New Collected Poems* by Iain Crichton Smith, published and used with permission by Carcanet Press Limited

p. 95 Song: 'The Padre', Written by: Chris Hoban, Publishing: MCPS/PRS, Taken from the album *Centenary: Words & Music of The Great War*, Performed by: Show of Hands;

p. 115 'Watching the Reapers' by Bai Juyi, translated by Arthur Waley, used by permission of the Estate of Arthur Waley;

p. 139 excerpt from *The Sweetshop Owner* by Graham Swift, published by Pan Macmillan, first published 1980 by Allen Lane

Cover image: nevodka/Shutterstock